Advance Praise for *The Golden Daughter*

"This is a powerful and cathartic story—full of emotion, discovery, and a history few have chosen to share. I couldn't stop reading."
—Anna Maria Tremonti

"Halina St. James uncovers through exhaustive research the painful story of Maria, her Ukrainian mother, who was kidnapped into slave labour at the hands of the Nazis. *The Golden Daughter* is a story first of survival in the face of unmatched brutality, but then so much more. Maria is a heroine, and so is Halina for unearthing her mother's story, not just for herself, but also now, through this remarkable book, for us, so we never forget what happened in the darkest of times and how they cast a shadow on almost everything that followed."
—Peter Mansbridge

"An unputdownable book about a mother who dies holding on to her secrets, and a daughter determined to uncover the truth. Using her well-honed investigative skills, Halina St. James patches together her mother's entire troubled life, including her time as a slave worker for the Nazis. While the discoveries are devastating, they also help Halina understand her mother's often puzzling lies and hurtful behaviour. An absorbing journey of hope, forgiveness, and finding family. A must-read."
—Marsha Skrypuch, author of *Making Bombs for Hitler* and the *Kidnapped from Ukraine* trilogy

"After finding her mother's letters, Halina St. James discovered a story of secrets, slavery, anger, and betrayal, as saviours became seducers, and vice versa. But, ultimately, *The Golden Daughter* is a story of survival."

—Wendy Mesley, journalist

"Halina St. James's lifelong curiosity and emotional pain drives her to seek a deeper appreciation of the failings of her ancestors, which also leads to thrilling connections only blood provides. *The Golden Daughter* is a beautifully shared mystery of this age when family secrets crumble because of scientific and information innovation, providing answers to the question: 'Who am I, really?'"

—Kevin Newman, journalist

"From the opening page, *The Golden Daughter* captivated my imagination and then seized my heart and soul. Although the characters in this tragic love triangle are crafted from personal and historical fragments, they are vivid, deeply human, and unforgettable. And Halina St. James's reflections at the end allow you to accompany her on a profound journey of healing and hope. This is a rare and precious gift of a book."

—Nancy Regan, author of *From Showing Off to Showing Up: An Impostor's Journey from Perfect to Present*

"In this deeply touching memoir, Halina St. James mines historical documents and archives, as well as the softest places of her heart, to empathically tell the story of her beautiful but damaged young mother. *The Golden Daughter* is part memoir and part a deeply researched historical retelling of one of the lesser-known atrocities visited upon eastern Europeans by the Nazis. This is St. James's heartfelt quest to come to terms with a deceptive and emotionally distant mother and find her lost father. It's an emotion-filled search for the understanding, belonging, and love for which she had always longed. It is the story of lives stolen, recovered, and finally reconciled—and ultimately, family love found."

—Pauline Dakin, author of *Run, Hide, Repeat: A Memoir of a Fugitive Childhood*

The Golden Daughter

MY MOTHER'S SECRET PAST
AS A UKRAINIAN SLAVE WORKER
IN NAZI GERMANY

HALINA ST. JAMES

ANANSI

Copyright © 2025 Halina St. James

Published in Canada and the USA in 2025 by House of Anansi Press Inc.
houseofanansi.com

All rights reserved. No part of this publication may be reproduced or transmitted in any form or by any means, electronic or mechanical, including photocopying, recording, or any information storage and retrieval system, without permission in writing from the publisher.

House of Anansi Press is committed to protecting our natural environment. This book is made of material from well-managed FSC®-certified forests, recycled materials, and other controlled sources.

House of Anansi Press is a Global Certified Accessible™ (GCA by Benetech) publisher. The ebook version of this book meets stringent accessibility standards and is available to readers with print disabilities.

29 28 27 26 25   1 2 3 4 5

Library and Archives Canada Cataloguing in Publication
Title: The golden daughter : my mother's secret past as a Ukrainian slave worker in Nazi Germany / Halina St. James.
Names: St. James, Halina, 1947- author.
Identifiers: Canadiana (print) 20250200937 | Canadiana (ebook) 2025020097X | ISBN 9781487013158 (softcover) | ISBN 9781487013165 (EPUB)
Subjects: LCSH: Brik, Maria. | LCSH: World War, 1939-1945—Conscript labor—Germany. | LCSH: Forced labor—Germany—History—20th century. | LCSH: St. James, Halina, 1947-—Family. | CSH: Ukrainian Canadian women—Biography. | CSH: Ukrainian Canadians—Biography. | LCGFT: Biographies.
Classification: LCC HD4875.G3 S7 2025 | DDC 940.54/05—dc23

Cover design: Alysia Shewchuk
Cover images: oleg7799/VectorStock.com; emybrook/VectorStock.com
Interior design and typesetting: Lucia Kim
Interior images: Author's collection

House of Anansi Press is grateful for the privilege to work on and create from the Traditional Territory of many Nations, including the Anishinabeg, the Wendat, and the Haudenosaunee, as well as the Treaty Lands of the Mississaugas of the Credit.

 Canada Council for the Arts   Conseil des Arts du Canada   ONTARIO ARTS COUNCIL CONSEIL DES ARTS DE L'ONTARIO

With the participation of the Government of Canada
Avec la participation du gouvernement du Canada | Canadä

We acknowledge for their financial support of our publishing program the Canada Council for the Arts, the Ontario Arts Council, and the Government of Canada.

Printed and bound in Canada

For the 5.7 million individuals whose youth was stolen from them, and whose lives were changed forever, when the Nazis forced them into slavery

And for their children and families, whose destinies were defined by what those wartime slaves endured

Contents

Author's Note xi
Prologue: For My Beautiful Mama 1

PART I: DESPAIR

Chapter 1: That Accursed Day 5
Chapter 2: The Brick Factory 12
Chapter 3: Slow Train to Hell 21
Chapter 4: OST 33
Chapter 5: 8 Schillerstrasse 42
Chapter 6: Chance Encounters 53
Chapter 7: Barracks, Ball Bearings, and Bombs . . . 63
Chapter 8: Freedom 69
Chapter 9: A Man You Can Trust 78
Chapter 10: Beginnings and Endings 91
Chapter 11: The Khaki Labyrinth 98
Chapter 12: Warning Signs 108
Chapter 13: Camp Hope 119

PART II: DECEPTION

Chapter 14: Timmins Triangle 129
Chapter 15: Alone at the Station 142
Chapter 16: War and Peace 150
Chapter 17: Fathers and Daughters 154
Chapter 18: Killarney 163
Chapter 19: A Tangled Web 173

PART III: DISCOVERY

Chapter 20: The Letters. 185
A Letter to Sergei 201
Chapter 21: Würzburg 203
Chapter 22: Schweinfurt 211
A Letter to Mama 218
Chapter 23: Weiden. 221
A Letter to Tata 231
Chapter 24: Bad Reichenhall 234
Chapter 25: Hopes and Dreams. 243
A Letter to Aniela 249
Chapter 26: Damn Polacks 251
Chapter 27: The Man in the Chateau. 264
A Letter to Stan 275
Chapter 28: Poland 277
A Letter to Ignacy and Józefa 291
Chapter 29: A Final Boo 294

Acknowledgements *301*

Author's Note

More than 5.7 million people were put to work as slaves in Germany by the Nazis. Most of them, like my mother, were taken against their will. Earlier, a few went willingly, lured by posters that promised food, money, and the chance to learn a trade.

All of them, the unwilling and the willing, became cogs in the German war machine. They were treated as subhuman, and many were worked to death.

My mother survived this horrendous period of history. But she rarely talked about it, and never in detail. I have reconstructed her life, not only from the secret letters and documents I found after her death, but also from the experiences of other survivors and their families.

I had the help of archivists, the encouragement of friends, and the support of strangers I met along the way. Understanding my mother's life as a slave helped me recognize how it impacted my own life.

Throughout this book I have stuck, as far as possible, to the historical facts and the available records. Some characters, actions, and conversations I have created, based on what I learned from the letters and my research.

What is not imagined, and continues to amaze me, is the resilience of those slave workers in Nazi Germany. Most of them are dead now. But even when they lived, many were unable—or unwilling—to speak of their experiences.

Like my mother, those slave workers, many no more than children, found the strength to survive at a time when the world went mad.

I celebrate them in these pages.

Prologue

For My Beautiful Mama

Who loved beauty and glamour
Who had dreams and plans
But whose life was changed forever
Stolen by a war she had no part of.

For my beautiful Mama
Who did the best she could
With her marriages, her child, her new country
Who kept surviving until she couldn't.

For my beautiful Mama
Who escaped a war
Who crossed an ocean
Who lost her dreams in foreign lands.

For my beautiful Mama
Who could never tell me her true story
Whose secrets are lost forever
So a part of me is lost too.

For my beautiful Mama
Whose story and secrets are safe now
Deep in the ocean she crossed carrying her dreams.
Now you can rest in peace, Mama.

PART I
DESPAIR

Chapter 1

That Accursed Day

February 24, 1943, started off as an ordinary day in Vinnytsia, Ukraine—if you can call living under a brutal regime "ordinary." The Nazis had captured the city in 1941, and they'd made their presence known: swastikas, soldiers, guns, and German shepherds—Hitler's favourite dog—were everywhere.

Sergei Brik went to work in the forest, just as he always did. Aniela Brik, his wife, a seamstress, stayed home, cutting out a dress for a client.

Every day, Sergei and Aniela debated whether they should send Maria, their only child, to school. She was seventeen years old, studying to be a pharmacist at the technicum, a post-secondary school. They had pulled strings to get her into the prestigious school, but during the war they knew there was a risk the school would be targeted by the Nazis, who were snatching people and forcing them to work in Germany.

Aniela didn't know, couldn't know, what was soon to happen. Years later, in a letter to Maria, she called February 24, 1943, "that accursed day." She made the decision: "Go to school, Musya," she said, using her pet name for Maria. "It's safe."

The school day started as they always did. Maria kissed Aniela goodbye, walked out the arched entrance to their apartment block, and turned left toward the technicum. She hugged her books close to her chest. It was cold. At the park at the end of her street, she met up with her two best friends, Lena and Valya. The girls chatted excitedly, happy to be together, to be going to school. With the war, and Nazi soldiers everywhere, the technicum was a welcome distraction, a bit of normal in a life that was far from normal. When they got to the school, they dashed inside, glad to be out of the winter wind. It was eight o'clock.

Maria, Lena, and Valya were sitting at their desks when they heard pounding on doors along the hallway. They looked at each other.

Their classroom door was suddenly flung open.

"What is the meaning of this!?" The teacher's question was ignored by the Nazis rushing to enter. They had rifles, clubs, and dogs.

"*Steh auf! Bewegen!*" the soldiers screamed.

Maria understood some German. She knew what they were shouting: *Get up! Move!*

The students scrambled from their desks, overturning chairs as the Nazis forced them into the hall. There was no time to put on winter coats. Some of the students were screaming, others crying. All were frightened.

They were pushed down the hall and through the technicum's main doors. A blast of cold air hit Maria. She and the others were thrust between two rows of SS soldiers. If anyone stopped or stumbled, they received the butt end of a rifle. Maria ran down the line as if her life depended on it. And it did.

Students and teachers alike were then forced into a fleet of open-backed trucks. Some of them tore their uniforms and stockings in the panic to get inside, lest they be hit. They were squeezed in, faces pressed into backs, unable to move, united in fear and confusion. Maria clung to the people around her, steadying herself as the truck bounced through the streets. She was packed in the middle. *At least here I can't feel the cold as much*, she thought.

Maria had been separated from Valya and Lena. She had no idea what was going on. She had no idea where she was being taken.

Everything changed on that accursed day.

AT HOME, ANIELA BENT over the dress, making sure she was cutting it straight. At ten o'clock, there was a pounding at the door. She dropped her scissors as her friend Anna burst into the apartment.

"Where is Maria?" Anna cried, her eyes darting anxiously around the room.

"At the technicum. Why?"

"Haven't you heard? They've surrounded the school."

Aniela looked at Anna in disbelief. The technicum! Surrounded by Nazis! No, this couldn't be true. Schools were supposed to be safe.

Aniela grabbed her coat and bolted out the door, forgetting her hat. When she got to the technicum, it was all over. The trucks were gone. A few soldiers were left to deal with anxious parents and relatives. She found out that Maria had been taken to a holding camp at the brick factory. When Aniela turned to go, a soldier stopped her with a gun to her chest.

Aniela stepped back. The soldier told her she had to stay at the technicum. The Nazis didn't want word of what had happened to get out. The students at the technicum had two shifts of classes—one at eight o'clock and the other at eleven. The second shift of students was expected, and the Nazis wanted to seize them too. But those students never came—because by then the whole city knew about the raid.

Aniela paced, trapped and helpless. She was in the school's office when Manya, the wife of a wealthy store owner and a client of Aniela's, walked in.

"What are you doing here?" asked Manya.

"They've taken Musya."

"Taken Musya? Why? Didn't you know that today is the twenty-fourth? They said they were going to take students today because they have to fill their quotas."

"No, I didn't know."

"Well, I did. I kept my Josef home."

Aniela couldn't believe what Manya was saying. She

had known the Nazis were going to the school and hadn't come to warn her? What kind of friend was this? *A bitch,* thought Aniela, *a damn bitch. And why is she here now? To see my pain, to gloat. What kind of mother would do this to another mother?* Aniela narrowed her eyes at Manya. In that moment she felt she could tear her apart.

Instead, Aniela turned away, drew a deep breath, and walked up to the first Nazi she saw. She was breathing hard. Her nose almost touching his, she focused her anger on his eyes.

"Where are you taking my daughter?"

"To work in medical care stations here in Ukraine," said the soldier. "It's okay. She's safe. She'll be home in two years."

Aniela held his eyes. He turned and walked away. Aniela collapsed in the nearest chair. All lies. Yet she wanted to believe them. The lies, no matter how feeble, were much better than the reality engulfing her family. They were pawns in this senseless chess game. They were expendable.

Oh God, please help Maria, thought Aniela.

At eleven o'clock the Nazis let the parents leave the school. Aniela ran toward the brick factory. Halfway there, she was stopped by an acquaintance going the other way. The woman was carrying a package. "Are you going to the brick factory?" she asked.

"Yes," panted Aniela. "What's going on?"

"Don't go. They're all locked up and no one can see them until three o'clock. We can give them packages then."

"Not until three?!"

"Yes. Three o'clock. It's a waste of time now. I tried. The pigs won't let them out. I have to go now and get ready. Good luck." With that, the woman hurried away.

Aniela turned and ran home. It was noon. She threw off her coat. She needed to prepare something for Maria. Where to start?

Oh God, oh God, help me, she prayed. *Please help me save my Musya.* Aniela thought about how she had always told Maria to get out of Ukraine if she had the chance. There was no future for her under the Communists. But not like this. Not into the arms of the Nazis. No, no, this was much worse than staying here. *Focus, Aniela*, she told herself. *Focus! What does Maria need now? Bread! Oh no, we don't have any bread.* There was no time to bake loaf bread, so Aniela did the next-best thing. She began making flatbreads, kneading the dough furiously. Aniela flew through the kitchen, then the bedroom, then the kitchen again. Cooking, packing. Her hair was a mess; tears streaked her face.

In the middle of this flurry, Sergei threw open the door to the apartment. He knew what had happened and started yelling at Aniela that it was her fault. He was pacing, pulling his hair, rubbing his eyes, weeping.

Aniela tried to touch Sergei, but he slapped her away. She wanted to comfort him. She wanted him to comfort her. Why was he blaming her?

"Sergei, please. Help me. We have to bring food and clothes to Musya. We don't have much time. Sergei, listen to me. Help me."

Sergei heard nothing. He fell to his knees, sobbing. His golden daughter, stolen from him. How could Aniela have let this happen?

At that moment, a neighbour rushed in. She had heard the news. She put half a kilogram of pork fat in Aniela's hand. Maria's favourite.

Aniela looked at her through red-rimmed eyes, flour on her face, a dishcloth in her hand. She let the neighbour steer her back into the kitchen, away from Sergei. The two women finished preparing the food and put it in a small suitcase. Then they filled the remaining space with clothes, pencils, paper, a comb, soap, a toothbrush—cramming in anything useful.

All the while, Sergei sat on the carpet and sobbed. Finally, he stood up, but he sagged like an old man. "Musin'ka, oh my golden Musin'ka," Sergei whispered, using his pet name for Maria.

Aniela went to him and took him in her arms. Slowly, he wrapped his arms around her. They stood holding each other, crying, but not for long.

"It's time to go," whispered Aniela.

Chapter 2

The Brick Factory

Aniela and Sergei hurried to the brick factory. They knew the evil that had been carried out there two years earlier. More than 350 Jews had been murdered by a Nazi killing squad, the Einsatzkommandos. The Jews had to dig a mass grave, and then they stood in it before the Nazis shot them. This was how the Nazis killed Jews before they industrialized the process with death camps.

The Pyatnichany Brick Factory was a perfect setting for these monstrous acts. Isolated, built around a quarry on the outer edge of the city, surrounded by barbed wire, it was an ideal holding camp for the students and teachers of the technicum.

Sergei, who was almost paralyzed when he heard the news of Maria's abduction, now ran down the street. His coat was open and flapping like wings around him, urging him to run faster and faster. Aniela was panting behind him, bundled in her winter coat. She was heavy, and sixty years old. Sergei was fifty-three and fit from working in the forest. He carried the small suitcase packed with food and clothes for Maria. His eyes stared straight ahead; he was willing the brick factory to come into view with every step. At the same time, he was dreading what he would find there.

They heard the noises first: screams, sobs, and cries for help, mingled with threats and dogs barking. When Aniela and Sergei finally got to the brick factory, they saw utter chaos. Crowds surged on both sides of the barbed-wire fence—students and teachers on one side, frantic relatives on the other. Watching everything and everyone were the SS soldiers and their dogs, unaffected by the tears and suffering. They were taught not to feel emotion for anything except Germany and its leader, Adolf Hitler. They were taught that everyone at the fence was inferior to them. They were taught to obey.

Aniela and Sergei pushed their way along the crowded fence, trying not to intrude on the painful partings occurring there. Many had found their loved ones, and they were weeping, poking fingers through the barbed wire. A touch. One more. A last touch.

Aniela and Sergei scanned the faces on the other side. "Musin'ka! Musya! Maria!" they cried over and over. They were almost at the end of the fence, and then—

"Mama! Papa!"

There she was, a vision that would haunt Sergei for the rest of his life. His darling Musin'ka was weeping bitterly, clutching a piece of black bread on the other side of the barbed-wire fence. Her hair hung limply behind her ears; her face was dirty and smeared by the tears streaking down to her chin. Her school uniform was filthy and torn. She was shivering.

Maria squeezed into a tiny space along the fence in front of Aniela and Sergei. They had come. Maybe, just maybe, they could do something—save her, get her out of this nightmare. She was so cold. She hadn't had time to grab her coat before the Germans took her.

"Papa, take me home. What's happening? Why am I here?"

"Shhh. Don't cry, Musin'ka," said Sergei. "I'm sure it's all a mistake. We'll get you out."

Aniela looked at him. She knew this was no mistake.

"They're putting us on a train tomorrow. We're supposed to go to Germany. I don't want to go to Germany!" Maria shouted.

An SS guard glanced at her.

"Shhh, Musya. Don't let them hear you," cautioned Aniela, smiling wanly at the guard. She was always the practical one, the cautious one.

"Here, my Musya, we have some clothes and food for you." Sergei threw the suitcase over the fence.

Maria stood still, staring at it. She frowned. Something was not right. Why were they throwing food and clothes at her when they were going to take her home? She looked at her parents. "You're not taking me home, are you?"

"You're cold. There's a sweater in the suitcase. Put it on," pleaded Aniela.

Maria looked at her mother. She looked at the suitcase again. If she took it, she would be admitting she was going to Germany. But if she didn't take it, she would be cold. And hungry. She had never been cold or hungry. Until now, she had never had to worry about anything, regardless of whether the Soviets or the Nazis ruled Vinnytsia.

Sergei and Aniela had spoiled her. She was their miracle child. They had thought they would never have children, but then, when Aniela was forty-two, Maria was born. Aniela and Sergei were overjoyed, not only to have this baby but to have such a beautiful baby.

Maria was their golden daughter in every sense—her blonde, almost platinum hair, her perfect features on her oval face. She rarely smiled, but that was fine. She had those beautiful, penetrating eyes. They were sad eyes, but that was fine too. Sergei and Aniela vowed to make their golden daughter happy. And they did, until that accursed day.

"Please, Musya," begged Aniela. "Put your sweater on."

Sergei started weeping.

"No! Not until you tell me what's going on. Why am I here?" Maria was almost screaming now.

"Shhh, please, Musya. Don't let them hear you. They told me at the school you are going to work in a medical centre. In Ukraine, not Germany." Aniela peered anxiously at Maria to see if she believed the lie, but she couldn't read anything on her daughter's face. "You'll learn about drugs and medicine, Musya. Isn't that nice?" she continued. "And then you'll be back in two years. Or maybe even less, who knows? But you'll be back before you know it.

This is hard now, I know, but think of it as an adventure. An education. You will be back. It's not forever." Aniela paused. "Please, Musya, put the sweater on."

"Musin'ka, listen to your mother, please. It will be all right," Sergei tried to reassure her.

Maria looked at her parents. Nothing about this felt all right. Her parents looked haggard, older than she had ever seen them. "Oh, Mama, Papa, please, please take me home," she begged, her defiance gone. She was their little girl. She needed her mother and father more now than she ever had in her life.

Aniela and Sergei wept helplessly in front of their daughter. The tears they had tried to hold back now flowed, and they clung together on their side of the fence. Then Sergei plunged his hand through the barbed wire. He felt no pain. Maria grabbed his hand and kissed it. He cupped her cheek, holding the sobbing Aniela in his other arm. They stood there weeping, a tragic tableau, one of many up and down the fence.

None of these scenes moved the Nazis. Somewhere along the fence somebody shouted an order. Dogs began snarling, and soldiers started forcing the students and teachers back inside the brick factory.

"Go, Musin'ka. Go. It will be okay," whispered Sergei.

"Mama, Papa, please, please don't leave me here." One last plea, and then a soldier shoved Maria toward the factory. She tried to run back to Aniela and Sergei, but the soldier hit her on the back with his rifle.

Aniela screamed, "No! Leave her alone!"

Maria stumbled. Hands helped her up. Someone picked up her suitcase. She disappeared inside the brick factory.

"We'll come tomorrow!" Sergei shouted, as Maria was led away. "To the train station."

"What time does the train leave?" Aniela cried to anyone who might be listening.

But no one was. Two guards positioned themselves in front of the factory door. Aniela and Sergei stood at the fence for a long time, weeping. They stood like the other grieving families, stunned at what had just happened.

"Come on, let's go," Sergei finally said, but Aniela wouldn't move. She just stood there, breathing hard, tears streaming down her cheeks. Maria was right there, just across the fence, a few steps away inside the brick factory, yet it was as if her Musya were on another planet. It was impossible for Aniela to help her. The insanity of this situation was unbearable.

She looked at the soldiers guarding the doors. "Pigs!" she screamed. "Pigs! You will burn in hell for this!"

The soldiers looked at them. Sergei grasped her by the shoulder. One took a step forward, readying his rifle.

"Shhh," Sergei murmured. At the same time, he turned her away from the fence. They began walking home, their feet dragging on the pavement, Sergei keeping his arm around Aniela all the way. No reason to hurry now.

Aniela had no idea how they got back to the apartment. They collapsed in their chairs. They didn't look at each other, didn't speak to each other. Each sat, unable to move, beaten, despair pinning them to their seats.

Finally, Aniela stood up. She was still wearing her coat and hat. "I'm going to find out when the train leaves."

Sergei didn't respond. He sat staring vacantly. After Aniela left, Sergei turned to the side table beside him and gazed dully at the three pictures there. In one, Maria was seven years old, her platinum-blonde hair cut in a short bob with bangs. She sat on a stool close to Sergei, wearing a pretty sleeveless summer dress. He was wearing a dark suit and tie. His face, like his daughter's, was oval, his short hair combed back off his high forehead and his moustache neatly trimmed. Father and daughter leaned toward each other, heads touching. He held her tight with one arm, her arm around his neck. It was not fashionable to smile in photographs, but Sergei couldn't suppress his. His pride in his golden daughter shone unashamedly for all to see. Maria gazed straight ahead, her eyes sad, her mouth turned down.

Sergei stared at the picture and burst into fresh tears. He could barely see the other photo, the one where Maria was a chubby four-year-old wearing an expensive chinchilla fur coat with a matching hat. She stood on an ornate table, holding a small shepherd's crook. Behind her stood Aniela, a portly woman dressed in a fur-trimmed coat and cloche hat. Maria's guardian angel. Aniela had a soft smile, but her eyes looked troubled. Maria, as always, stared unsmiling into the camera.

Sergei picked up the last photo, his favourite. Maria was five years old, standing alone on a chair. She was wearing a dark belted tunic with a white collar. Part of her blonde hair was gathered into a little ponytail on the top of her head, held in place with a big bow. Her ponytail showered her head like a fountain of gold. No smile here, either, and such sadness in her eyes.

The picture slipped out of Sergei's fingers and crashed to the floor, the glass in the frame breaking. "Oh, Musin'ka, Musin'ka. My golden Musin'ka." He remembered how Maria used to riffle through his pockets when he came home. She was so little she had to balance on her tiptoes, stretching his coat pocket open with one hand while she hunted for the treat with the other. Usually Sergei brought her a pastry. He knew he spoiled her, but he couldn't help it. She was so beautiful.

Aniela had been beautiful too. She'd had many suitors, but it was the young Sergei Brik who captured her heart.

"I'm too old for you," she had said. "People will talk."

"Let them. I don't care," Sergei declared. "I love you so much. You are my angel."

Aniela loved his passion, and his practical approach to life. Sergei had attended the same school in Odessa as Leon Trotsky, one of the leaders in the Russian Revolution of 1917. The school focused on the application of business and philosophical theories. Aniela had known Sergei would be a good provider.

As the years passed, Sergei had always told her the age difference didn't matter, but it did to Aniela. Although she had passed her childbearing years, she knew Sergei wanted a child, and so did she. When the miracle happened, Aniela was forty-two.

Maria was the greatest gift she could have given Sergei. What did it matter if he was now more smitten with his daughter than with his wife? What did it matter that he spoiled the child? Aniela provided the counterbalance, lovingly, firmly.

As Aniela rushed to the train station to get information, she wondered how her golden daughter would cope with whatever was in store for her. Had she prepared Maria for the hellish world that was Central Europe in 1943? Aniela knew, deep in her heart, that the answer was no. In her own way, she too had spoiled Maria, protecting her daughter from the realities of life that Maria needed to understand to survive in the world.

What Aniela didn't know was that a fighting spirit had been awakened in her golden daughter that day in the brick factory. It would shape the rest of Maria's life.

Chapter 3

Slow Train to Hell

At the end of that accursed day in the brick factory, hate, frustration, and fear wormed their way into Maria's heart. Why was this happening to her? She had always obeyed the Nazis' stupid rules. It wasn't fair that she was taken. She hated the Nazis.

Maria calmed herself down. That kind of thinking would get her nowhere. She assessed the situation. She couldn't escape. She was a prisoner, at least for the time being. So, no more "I don't want to go to Germany" outbursts. Too dangerous now. She watched the soldiers and their dogs carefully. Her eyes narrowed, trying to pick up clues about what would happen next.

Maria was a spoiled princess, but she was a smart spoiled princess. Her youth, hopes, and dreams had been wrenched from her in minutes, but she would be patient. Watching, waiting, not attracting attention—yes, that was the way to go.

"I think this is yours." A woman tapped Maria on the shoulder and handed her a suitcase.

"Oh, yes. It's mine. Thank you so much." Maria hadn't been able to pick it up when the soldiers pushed her into the brick factory. She had forgotten about it.

The woman nodded and moved on. Maria almost cried. She hadn't expected any acts of kindness in this nightmare. Maria knelt down and opened the suitcase, took out a sweater and put it on. She noticed the food Aniela had packed. *Better not to eat it now, she reasoned.* Who knew when she would really need food.

The Nazis had given them a piece of dry bread and a cup of fake coffee made from a mixture of chicory, soybeans, barley, grain, and acorns. Maria was still hungry, but she could wait. She picked up her suitcase and wandered around, looking for Valya and Lena.

Valya was her cousin and Lena was their friend. The three girls were the same age. Growing up together, they had been inseparable. There was a picture of them at Maria's house—sweet young faces, sixteen years old, on the brink of becoming women. They were dressed in their school uniforms—white blouses with white sailor collars, white ribbons in their hair. The three girls were sitting together: Valya in the centre, her dark hair in long braids, with Lena and Maria leaning toward her on either side. Maria's hair was short and dark, the golden tresses left behind in childhood. Valya had a wry smile on her face, while Lena, a real Slavic beauty, smiled softly. As always, Maria did not smile; she stared straight ahead, her eyes sad. They were all so innocent, facing the camera confidently, ignorant of what awaited them.

Maria searched the brick factory for her friends. The room was huge. Bricks were stacked along one wall. The floor was packed earth. Carts and tools were scattered around. The few tall windows were covered in grime, but a bit of light managed to seep in, highlighting the dust that hung everywhere, blanketing the bricks, the tools, even the cobwebs. Even though the students and teachers had been there only a few hours, they were covered in dust too. They milled around in small groups, clutching their possessions, talking in hushed voices, heads down, glancing furtively at the guards. In the disappearing daylight, this miserable clutch of humanity looked like the walking dead.

At last, Maria spotted Valya and Lena. They were sitting under one of the windows, Valya holding Lena. Maria ran to them. The girls embraced, weeping in each other's arms. They huddled together on the floor. The factory was unheated, and there were only a few lights, bare bulbs hanging from the ceiling on long cords. Maria looked up to see the last rays of daylight struggling in through the grubby windows.

"What do you think will happen to us?" whispered Lena.

"I don't know," Valya whispered back. "Someone told me we're going to Germany."

"No," said Maria. A guard looked at her. Maria lowered her voice. "We're going to work in a medical centre in Ukraine. Mama told me."

"Oh, Maria, how would she know?" snapped Valya. "She probably told you that story so you wouldn't be afraid."

"Well, where do you think we're going?" Maria was used to Valya's outbursts.

"To hell," whispered Lena. The girls looked at her and fell silent, lost in their own thoughts.

"I'm hungry," said Maria eventually. "I've got some food."

"I've got some food too," said Valya, reaching for the pillowcase behind her, which her parents had stuffed with food and clothes.

"I have nothing," said Lena. Her parents hadn't been at the fence. There was no package of food for her, no clothes.

"It's okay, Lena," said Maria. "We'll share everything with you. Don't worry."

"But we have to be careful," said Valya. "We don't know what's going to happen, so we should ration our food, okay? Who knows how long we'll be on that train." She paused. "Wherever it's going."

They ate a small portion of the pork belly Aniela had packed and half a slice of bread Valya's mother had made, and then they put the suitcase and pillowcase against the wall. They leaned against them, just like in the photograph: Valya in the centre, Maria on the left, and Lena on the right. Only this time, there were no smiles, and there was no hope in their eyes.

They tried to sleep, but it was hard. Not only were there students and teachers from the technicum in the factory, but the Nazis had rounded up others from the town. People began settling and lying down. Soon, the night was filled with their whispering, crying, cursing, praying.

The guards were everywhere. They snaked their way among the prisoners, their boots raising dust from the floor, their rifles tight against their chests, their dogs padding obediently beside them. The guards weren't interested in the conversations, the pleading eyes, the worried looks around them. They had a job to do. The sooner they did it, the better.

Maria watched them. Then her eyes would close, but not for long. She woke up several times. Each time, the soldiers were there, watching them. *How can they stay awake all night?*

Valya slept fitfully too. When she and Maria were awake together, they would exchange glances, too scared to speak. Lena slept through the night, her head in Valya's lap. For Maria and Valya, the night confirmed what they knew in their hearts. They were prisoners. There would be no happy ending for them.

Finally, daylight began seeping through the windows. Maria and Valya sat up, looked around, and shook Lena awake. They were freezing.

Maria stopped a passing guard. "*Bitte, toilette?*" she asked.

The guard pointed his rifle toward a far corner of the brick factory.

Maria looked where he had pointed, but she was confused. "*Bitte, toilette?*" she asked again.

"*Dort! Geh dorthin!*" shouted the soldier, pointing his rifle to the corner again. *There! Go there!*

Lena and Valya shrank behind Maria, their eyes wide.

Maria squinted. At the far end of the factory, she saw a pile of straw. She gasped. There were people squatting in the straw. That explained the smell she had noticed when she woke up. Surely the guard didn't expect them to go there? In front of everyone?

The guard stood over the girls, an ugly grin on his face. He was enjoying their dilemma. It was always the same with these *untermenschlichs*, these subhumans. They were always shocked to learn their true place in society.

The girls walked to the corner under the watchful eyes of the soldier. As they got closer, Maria held her breath as long as she could. Then a quick gulp of air, and she held her breath again. The stench was awful. The girls looked in vain for a clean spot, away from other people. This was one time Maria wished she were a boy.

Finally, they found a spot. They relieved themselves and hurried back to their place under the window. Lena was crying softly, mortified that she had been forced to lift her skirt before an audience of soldiers, students, teachers, and strangers. Valya didn't care who saw what. She comforted Lena. Maria watched the soldiers. What were these monsters going to do with them?

They were given some weak fake coffee and dry black bread again. The girls devoured it. They didn't have much time.

"*Steh auf! Bewegen!*" the soldiers started hollering. *Get up! Move!* They motioned toward the door with their rifles. The factory door opened, letting in a blast of icy air. Maria snatched her suitcase, and Valya grabbed her pillowcase. Lena squeezed herself in between Maria and Valya.

Again, the girls had to run between two rows of soldiers. Again, they had to climb into open-backed trucks. Again, questions, crying, slowness were rewarded with the butt end of a rifle. Maria, Valya, and Lena ran together so they wouldn't be separated, and managed to get on the same truck. They clung to one another, swaying in the cold February morning, trying to stay upright.

Maria observed the landmarks as they rattled by. "We're going to the train station."

"Maybe our parents will come and save us," offered Lena.

"I wouldn't count on it," snorted Valya.

Maria, Lena, and Valya were pushed out of the truck toward a cattle car. Each of the train's wooden wagons had soldiers with rifles and dogs standing at the doors. The soldiers pushed and kicked the prisoners inside. The scene was chaotic. Soldiers shouting, dogs barking. The relatives, held back from the cattle cars, were screaming, crying, pleading, begging. All in vain.

Maria looked around in this sea of madness. Where were her parents? She clutched Lena's coat, while Lena grasped Valya's coat. With their free hands, the girls tried to protect the suitcase and pillowcase as they were pushed toward a cattle car. But in the melee, Valya lost her pillowcase.

The girls got on the train quickly. They were terrified the soldiers would hit them or the dogs bite them. They half crawled, half jumped into the cattle car, all the time pushed by others struggling behind them, everyone afraid of being trampled.

The Nazis continued shoving, pushing, and beating everyone into the train. Some parents broke through the line of soldiers. They reached for their children, only to be forced back by a blow from a rifle.

The girls managed to get into the same train car. They stood together until their car was full. Then the door slid shut. They heard the heavy thud of a bar outside, locking them in.

Inside, it was dark, with only a hint of light seeping in through cracks in the wooden slats. Everyone was quiet, listening to the muffled mayhem outside. Once, there was banging on their door, then a cry, then no more banging.

Finally, the train started to roll forward. Valya and Lena began to cry. Maria stared ahead, her eyes dry. Oh, how she hated the Nazis. No way was she going to give them the satisfaction of crying.

ANIELA AND SERGEI HAD spent a sleepless night at home in their apartment after Aniela had come back from her search for answers.

"Nobody knows anything, but Valentina at City Hall told me a train would be leaving around eight o'clock," Aniela reported. "We have to be there, Sergei."

Sergei looked at his wife through red-rimmed eyes. He couldn't help but think this was all her fault. She hadn't protected their golden daughter. Now his precious Musin'ka was lost. He began to cry again.

"Sergei! Listen to me. We have to go to the train station. Now!"

Sergei had spent the night in his chair in the same clothes he had worn the day before, his hair dishevelled, his face unshaven. His eyes were puffy and bloodshot.

"Please, Sergei. It's getting late. We have to go. Do this for Musya."

Sergei sat up. Maybe, just maybe, they could grab his Musin'ka at the train station. Run away with her. It was crazy, but he had to try. Sergei got up, blew his nose, and followed Aniela out the door. They ran to the Vinnytsia train station, but they were too late.

By the time Aniela and Sergei got to the train station, they were swept into a sea of misery much worse than at the fence the day before. Parents and relatives, sobbing, some on their knees weeping, others running along the railway tracks until they could run no more. Then they collapsed, crying in anguish.

Aniela and Sergei looked frantically for the train. "The train. Where's the train?" screamed Aniela. She grabbed hold of strangers' coats, their arms, anything to get their attention, yelling her question at them.

Finally someone answered. "Too late. Too late. They're gone."

Aniela looked at the railway tracks. In the distance

she could make out a plume of smoke. Sergei reached her side. She looked at him and pointed down the tracks, tears streaming down her face.

"No!" shouted Sergei. He started to run down the tracks. "Musin'ka! Musin'ka!"

Aniela ran after him. Finally, he could run no more. Sergei fell to his knees. He thought his heart was going to burst. He hung his head, trying to breathe. His hands were on the tracks as he tried to support himself.

Aniela came up beside him. He wrapped his arms around her legs. She bent over him, sobbing. Slowly, she fell to her knees beside him. They held each other as the plume of smoke disappeared from view.

A soldier came up behind them. "*Steh auf! Geh!*" Get up! Go! Other soldiers started driving people away from the station.

Aniela and Sergei helped each other up. Aniela's dress was torn, her hat askew. Sergei's trousers were ripped at the knees. They heard the orders the soldiers screamed out, but they didn't react. They were numb. The Nazis could do what they wanted with them. What was there to live for now? Maria was gone, who knew where. Aniela and Sergei stumbled home, dazed, heartbroken.

AS THE TRAIN LEFT Vinnytsia behind, people started to stake out their standing room in the car. Maria noticed they were standing in straw. She felt something sticking to her shoe.

"What's this?" she asked, lifting her foot up.

A voice in the darkness piped up. "Our cows were here. The Nazis took them all to Germany, then they sent the train back for us. Our cows left a few presents behind because they didn't like going to Germany. We're the cows now."

Only a few people laughed.

As Maria's eyes adjusted to the dimness, she could see the others, her unlucky companions. The train rolled on. There was nothing in the wagon, just straw and filth. The girls lost count of how many days they stood, unable to sit or lie down, leaning on each other, leaning on strangers.

They had eaten all their food what seemed like ages ago. They were hungry, thirsty, and so cold. Early in their journey one of the women used the thick heel of her boot to bang a hole in one of the floorboards. Everyone used that hole as the toilet as the train rumbled on. With each kilometre, the cattle car smelled worse and worse.

Finally, the train stopped. Everyone waited anxiously, all eyes on the door. They were filthy, sleep-deprived, hungry, and thirsty. Their clothes were torn, dirty, and covered in straw, some smeared with excrement. They looked like the subhumans the Nazis said they were.

There was noise outside. A man looked through the slats of the cattle car. "We're at a station," he announced. "I can see the SS."

An ominous thud. The door slid open. Light poured into the cattle car. The wretched human cargo stared out, blinking and wiping their eyes.

Maria stood on her tiptoes and craned her neck to see above her companions. The sign at the train station said *Neumarkt*.

She was in Germany.

Chapter 4

OST

With the cattle car door open, the human cargo instinctively huddled closer together. The in-rush of fresh air was intoxicating, a welcome relief from the fetid atmosphere of the wagon, but the light was blinding after days in the dark.

Maria couldn't stop blinking and rubbing her eyes. Slowly, she was able to bring the scene in front of her into focus. Lena, Valya, and the others crowded beside her. Nazis with guns and dogs stood in front of them.

"*Raus! Raus!*" the Nazis started shouting at them. *Go! Go!*

The girls stumbled off the train, stunned, their legs stiff from standing. Many of the others fell onto the platform and had to crawl before they could get their legs to work.

Maria looked around. "No trucks."

"Maybe we're going inside the train station," said Lena, shivering.

"Ha!" scoffed Valya. "I doubt it."

"I'm so cold and tired and hungry," moaned Lena. "I can't remember the last time we ate."

"Shhh," soothed Maria. "We'll get some food soon. At least we're together."

"Yeah, we're together," muttered Valya. "For now."

They were herded into a column, and the chain of human misery began plodding forward. They left the station and walked along a wide street lined with houses, two or three storeys high, painted in crayon colours: red, blue, yellow, green. Happy, colourful homes. Each sloping roof was shaped and trimmed differently. Some had what looked like steps from the top to the bottom, trimmed in white. Others had white curlicue twists and turns. The street belonged in a fairy tale. People were stopping in their tracks to stare.

"Mama, look!" A little boy pointed at them, his cheeks rosy from the cold. He was bundled up like a little dumpling. His mother shushed him, drawing him close as the human chain shuffled by.

Maria looked up to see people in the windows. What did they think of this sad procession blighting their quaint Bavarian city?

Soon, the buildings gave way to fields. Still, they trudged on.

"Look," said Valya.

The girls craned their necks. They could see a barbed-wire fence, watchtowers, and an entrance guarded by soldiers. As the line the girls were in shuffled through,

Maria could see rows of wooden barracks. The girls were steered into one, a large room with rows of rough wooden bunks, three beds one on top of the other. There were no ladders to get to the top two beds. A passageway the width of a person ran between the canyon of bunks. A small stove stood at one end, barely heating a quarter of the room. No mattresses, no bedding, not even straw. There was one filthy, stinking toilet bucket by the entrance.

"Come on," said Valya. "Let's get a bunk near the stove."

Everyone had the same idea. The girls were too slow and had to settle for a bunk beyond the meagre circle of warmth, but at least it was a bottom bunk, so they didn't have to climb up.

Lena lay down, curled in the fetal position, and began to cry. Valya lay down beside her, folded her arms on her chest, and fell asleep. Maria put her suitcase at the head of the bunk, crawled in beside Valya and reached over to stroke Lena's back. When her friend stopped sobbing and her breath was even, Maria stretched out, resting her head on her suitcase. The three girls huddled together for warmth.

Maria couldn't see much of the room from her bunk, but she could hear people jostling for space, three or four to a bed. She listened to people groaning in the other bunks, trying to get comfortable on the cold wooden boards. She heard the sound of urine and feces splashing into the toilet bucket. She heard the sobbing, the words shared in hushed, worried voices, and the snoring. Then everyone was quiet. Maria tried to sleep, but she couldn't. She felt so weak. Yet she must have fallen asleep because before she knew it light was slipping in through the windows of the barracks.

Soldiers came in with hard bread and watery soup.

"What is this?" asked Lena, flicking something floating in her soup.

"I don't know," replied Maria, sniffing her bowl. "But it looks disgusting." She stirred her soup and gasped. "There's nothing here but water and this stuff—I think it's potato skin. I don't think the potatoes were washed, either," she said, as she peered down at the dirt at the bottom of her bowl.

Valya, meanwhile, was downing spoonful after spoonful. "Eat up, girls. It's better than nothing. Sop it up with the bread and it'll be soft enough to chew. Who knows when the next meal will come."

Maria and Lena realized Valya was right. They ate, and then they waited. The Nazis came back, ordering them to take their belongings and form a line, marching them to a bigger building where they were called forward one at a time. The Nazis hung a piece of cardboard with a number around each person's neck. They took their pictures, fingerprinted them, and registered them in a thick black ledger. The process was quick and efficient. Frighteningly so, thought Maria. How many other souls had stood in line like her, waiting for their lives to be set on a new course, or perhaps ended? She shivered.

Afterward, the girls huddled together, waiting again. An SS officer marched into the room. "Everybody remove your clothes!"

The three girls stared in disbelief. Did he want them to undress? Here? In a room full of their classmates, teachers, and strangers, men and women? No, that was not possible.

"Strip!" snapped the officer. "Now! And leave your clothes and anything else in this room."

Guards moved among the crowd, slapping people indiscriminately with sticks or rifles. Lena started to sob. Maria and Valya gritted their teeth. When the girls were naked, they stood close together, trying to cover their bodies, trying to salvage a shred of humanity from this humiliation.

People were being led in small groups through the door. When it was their turn, guards motioned for them to stand in front of a table. A Nazi soldier not much older than them, pen poised over a black ledger, stared at them.

Two men and a woman in white coats, masks, and latex gloves were in the room. After days in the cattle cars, most of the prisoners were weak, sick, and covered in lice.

"Spread your legs," said one of the men. Maria stared at him, terrified. "Spread your legs. Now!"

Still standing, she spread her legs. The doctor put a mirror with a long handle between her thighs. With his other hand, he used a stick to probe her genitals as he looked in the mirror. Maria's face burned.

The doctor said something to the clerk, who wrote in the ledger. As soon as the doctor removed the mirror, Maria clamped her legs together. Any minute now, she thought, she would wake up in her bed and Aniela would bring her some sweet tea with a slice of lemon.

Next the other male doctor studied Maria. She composed herself and met his eyes. Did she see a flicker of pity there? He didn't say anything, just motioned with his stethoscope for her to drop her arms. He listened to her chest, then motioned for her to turn around and listened to her back, checking her lungs for tuberculosis. She turned to face him again, her hands protecting her breasts. She looked at him carefully. There it was again. A flicker of pity, a sign of humanity. She wasn't mistaken. He saw her, in that brief second, as a human being. Maria hung her head in shame. Then he was gone to the next person.

The woman was last. Maria searched her eyes. Her face was impassive as she assessed Maria. "Show me your teeth."

Maria bared her teeth.

"Show me your hands."

Maria held out her hands.

The doctor looked without touching. "Hmmm, not much hard work." She looked up at Maria. "What did you do at home?"

"I was a student."

"What were you studying?"

"Pharmacology."

The doctor turned to the soldier with the ledger, said a few words, and then turned back to Maria. "Go through that door."

Maria glanced at Valya and Lena. They were still being examined. Lena was sobbing as the doctor poked and prodded her with his stick. It was the same stick he used for the men, lifting their penis and testicles, probing their pubic hair for bugs.

Maria bit her lips to keep from screaming. She was led to a large communal washroom. A soldier motioned to some birch-tar soap that had been used so often it was nothing more than a sliver. It kept slipping from Maria's fingers as she washed in the cold shower. The soldier laughed. After her shower, Maria was left standing and shivering with others. There were no towels.

One of the guards approached the group with a long, thin canister with a pump. "Stand straight," he ordered. Maria looked at him apprehensively. The guard pumped the canister vigorously and started spraying down the line. Maria was covered head to toe in a fine powder. She coughed, trying not to inhale the powder.

Finally, she was taken back to the main room. She was shivering uncontrollably. Her suitcase lay open on the floor, her clothes spilling out. She reached to pick them up, then stopped, trying to figure out what she was smelling.

"They sprayed everything for bugs," said a teacher. "Just flap your clothes around and put them on. Don't look for the clothes you were wearing. They burned them."

"Why?" stammered Maria.

"Bugs, infection. They think we'll make them sick."

Maria put on as many clothes as she could to stay warm. Valya and Lena stumbled into the room naked, covered in the DDT powder. Valya was holding Lena, who was almost hysterical, covering her head with her arms.

Valya stared at Maria, her eyes dead. Maria took a step back and stifled a cry. Valya's beautiful long braids had been hacked off. Her hair was a jagged mess, sticking up all over her head. Valya nodded at Lena.

Maria gasped as Lena lowered her arms, still weeping. She was almost bald, tufts of hair here and there, her scalp bleeding in places. Lena's pride and joy had been her long, glossy, thick hair. Now it was all gone. The girls held each other and cried.

"They told me I had bugs," said Lena, between sobs.

"They said my braids were too long," said Valya.

Where was her fiery Valya? Maria held both girls tightly.

"Why didn't they cut your hair?" asked Valya.

"I don't know," replied Maria. "They checked my head and sprayed it and let me go. Come on, let's get dressed. I have enough clothes for you both."

Maria gave Lena a woollen knitted hat that Aniela had made. By the time they were dressed, Maria's suitcase was empty. They had eaten all the food long ago. Maria closed her last link to home and left it on the floor.

Soldiers entered the room and gave everyone a safety pin and a small patch of blue cloth with white letters that spelled OST.

Valya stared at hers. "What does this mean?" she whispered to Maria.

Maria shrugged.

"Pin these to your outer clothes on the right side. Just here," ordered a soldier, pointing to his right breast. "Now you are all Ostarbeiter. Our honoured workers from the east," he sneered. "Never, ever go anywhere without your badge. You could be shot. Let's go."

The girls were led through another gate in a barbed-wire fence guarded by a watchtower. They entered another barracks, laid out just like the first. They claimed a bunk. Again they were lucky and didn't have to climb over other bunks. There was one guard. He looked kind.

Maria plucked up her courage. "Please. What's happening? Where are we?"

The soldier studied her. "You are at the Wolfstein Transit Camp for workers. You are on the clean side now. Before you were on the unclean side. You will wait here for further orders."

"How long?"

"As long as it takes." He turned and left.

That was why, Maria realized, they had been processed, sanitized, and labelled. They were going to work in Germany. Not in a medical facility in Ukraine as Aniela had told her. Probably not for two years, either.

Maria looked at her chest. The OST badge taunted her. She struck her chest hard with her open hand, covering the badge. She narrowed her eyes. She would survive. Somehow, she would survive.

Chapter 5

8 Schillerstrasse

Two weeks later, Maria, Valya, and Lena were marched back to the train station and thrust into another cattle car. But unlike the one that had brought them to Germany, this one had no straw on the floor. It had no toilet hole, either. Maria worried because she was menstruating.

The three friends huddled together, rocking gently with the motion of the train. Their companions in the cattle car were all from the Wolfstein Transit Camp. Everyone had been photographed, sanitized, and recorded in the German ledgers. They had been taken to barracks on the clean side of the camp and told to wait. Now, they were told, they would find out exactly how they would serve the Reich.

The girls were wearing the same clothes they had put on after those humiliating showers, and they hadn't had another shower since. They lived and slept in their clothes, managing only to wash their underwear occasionally. They looked and smelled wretched. The OST badge pinned over their right breast stood out like a neon sign, labelling them as subhumans for all to see.

Valya's hair was still a jagged mess. She didn't care and held her head up defiantly. Lena kept Maria's hat clamped on her naked head. Maria checked her scalp and body daily for bugs. The camp had been crawling with them.

"God," said Valya, as the train rounded a curve, throwing the girls together, "I hope the food is better where we're going. No damn bugs!"

"Ach, I just want some real bread," sighed Maria. "None of that crap filled with sawdust. Do they really think we don't know?"

"Why do they treat us like this?" whispered Lena. "What have we done to deserve this? We're human beings, just like them."

"Well, they don't think so," retorted Valya. "We're nothing to them, and you'd better get used to that; otherwise, you won't survive."

Lena burst into tears. "I want to go home."

Maria put her arm around her. "You will go home. This has to end at some point. The war can't go on forever." She looked pointedly at Valya.

"Hmph," muttered Valya.

Lena pulled away from Maria. "Do you think they told us the truth when they said this trip wasn't going to take too long?"

"Who knows?" replied Valya.

When the girls found out they were leaving the camp, Maria had looked for the guard with the kind face. "I'm going to Würzburg soon. To work for a doctor's family. Please, is Würzburg far from here?" she'd asked when she found him.

"Not far," said the guard. "Maybe two or three hours by train. Doctor's house, yeah?"

"Yeah."

"Good." Then he walked away.

Maria was left wondering what he meant. Good that it was a doctor? Good that it was Würzburg? She told the girls what the guard had said.

"What does that mean?" asked Lena.

"Who knows? I don't trust anything those Nazis tell me."

"Do you know anything about the doctor you're going to work for?" asked Lena. She had been assigned as a housemaid in another doctor's house.

"No. What about you?"

"Well, he's a doctor, but they also said he and his brother own a big department store in Würzburg. That's all I know," said Lena with a shrug.

"Well, I'm going to work in a bakery," said Valya. "And guess what I'm gonna do first?" She mimed stuffing a pastry into her mouth, smacking her lips and rolling her eyes in ecstasy. "And I bet they won't have bugs or sawdust in their precious German bakery."

"Just make sure you don't eat everything," laughed Maria. "Save some goodies for us when we come to visit. I hope we can," she added, smiling at Valya.

Valya hugged her. "I'll make sure I save the best for you."

"Oh, I hope they're all nice to us," sighed Lena, picking at the OST badge on her chest.

"I don't care about them being nice," said Valya. "I'm going to get everything I can out of them. I hate the Nazis."

Maria didn't say anything. She was wondering how she, who had never done a single bit of housework in her entire life, had been assigned to work as a housemaid for a doctor. Most of the others were going to work on farms or in factories, or doing other manual labour.

The girls were lost in their thoughts as the train rolled to Würzburg, to their uncertain future. Maria stared absently at her hands. Of course, she thought, that's why she was going to be a housemaid. She didn't have a worker's hands. Hers were soft, with no calluses. That female doctor at the transit camp had taken note.

The train arrived in Würzburg the same day. Once again, they formed a column. They walked in silence down a cobblestone path leading into the city, sometimes slipping on the uneven surface.

It was late afternoon on a warm spring day in March. Würzburg was older, bigger than Neumarkt. Maria saw grand buildings with ornate decorations, some with domes and columns. But all she could think of was food. She was weak. She needed to eat. Would her new employers be kind? How many children did they have? Would they feed her real food? She craved bread with sweet butter, topped with a thick slice of pan-fried pork belly.

After what seemed like hours of walking, the column

arrived at the Würzburg employment office. Maria learned the name of her employer: Dr. Horst Schroeder.

Lena was assigned to Dr. Rudoff Seisser, part of a wealthy business family. Valya went to the Zeppelinstrasse bakery in a part of town called Frauenland—women's land—because so many nuns lived there.

The girls were to be placed in roughly the same area, so soldiers took them all in the same truck to their new employers. They drove Maria to her employer's house first at 8 Schillerstrasse, a tall creamy-yellow building, four storeys high, standing on a corner. The top two floors had glass doors leading out to ornate wrought-iron balconies.

Maria and a guard climbed six steps to the front door. The guard rang the bell. Eventually, a woman opened the door. Maria gaped at her. She was the most beautiful thing Maria had ever seen. She was tall and slim. Maria knew from reading the fashion magazines her mother would get from influential clients that the woman was dressed in the latest French fashion, not the German fashion approved by the Nazis. She was wearing a dark-grey woollen skirt, slightly flared with pleats in the front, and a cream-coloured silk blouse fastened at the wrists with pearl buttons. Around her waist she had a wide belt in the same fabric as the skirt. The outfit was completed by a robin's egg–blue sweater casually thrown over her shoulders. It showed off her blue eyes.

But what fascinated Maria most was her face. The woman was beautiful. Her blonde hair was pulled away from her forehead and coiled into a heavy braid around her head. Red lipstick accented her full mouth. Her eyelashes were darkened with mascara. Her brows were plucked and pencilled in. To Maria, she was a goddess. Maria couldn't take her eyes off her. Neither could the guard, who suddenly became tongue-tied. The woman paid him no attention. She glanced at the papers he offered, signed them, and turned to Maria.

The guard bowed his head and left. Maria turned and waved goodbye to Lena and Valya as the truck drove off. How would they find each other again? Maria was overcome with sadness and anxiety. What was going to happen to her without her friends? She bit her lip to stop the tears. No, she wasn't going to show any feelings. The woman watched Maria coolly. Maria lowered her head. She knew how she looked with her soiled clothes, unkempt hair, dirty hands, and torn stockings. She knew she smelled.

The woman sighed. "I'm Frau Schroeder. You will work for me. Come."

Maria followed the woman inside, up a flight of stairs. Frau Schroeder opened a door that led to a long hallway. To the left, Maria saw an archway leading to an elegant living room with plum-coloured chairs and a sofa, dominated by a portrait of Hitler above an ornate fireplace.

Frau Schroeder led her briskly down the hall, past a couple of bedrooms, a room that Maria learned later was Dr. Schroeder's study, and the kitchen. The hallway ended in a pantry area behind the kitchen. Through it was a door. Frau Schroeder opened it.

"This is your room."

It was a tiny closet with a single bed and chest of drawers. No windows, but it was clean, with clean linens on the bed. Maria longed to throw herself on the bed and sleep.

Frau Schroeder walked around Maria slowly. To Maria's chagrin, Frau Schroeder was sniffing her. Maria cringed, aware of her body odour.

"Are you menstruating?" Frau Schroeder asked.

"Yes."

"What are you using? Rags?"

"Yes."

"How many do you have?"

"Just one."

"The one you have on you now?"

"Yes."

Frau Schroeder sighed again. "Take off all your clothes and put them here," she said, holding up an old pillowcase hanging on the inside doorknob. "You will wash everything before you wear them in the house. It's late today, so you will do laundry tomorrow. Understood?" Frau Schroeder spoke quietly, matter-of-factly.

Maria nodded. She had never washed clothes in her life. She was wondering what to do when Frau Schroeder spoke again.

"I will bring a bag for your rag. I will put it in the garbage, and I will give you clean rags. Never wash your rags or your clothes with Dr. Schroeder's and mine. Understood?"

Maria nodded.

"There is a toilet and sink off the kitchen for you to

use. Keep them clean. In the back of the pantry there's a tin washtub, washboard, and soap. You will use that for laundry and to wash yourself. You will wash yourself every day. I don't want any bugs or diseases in my house. Understood?"

Maria nodded enthusiastically. She wanted to keep clean.

"Now get the tub and put it in the kitchen behind the stove. I have hot water for you on the stove. Fill the tub and bathe yourself. Clean the tub and put it back when you're finished. I will put clean clothes in your room. Understood?"

Maria nodded and Frau Schroeder left. Washing herself in the small round tub with no one watching was pure joy. It was warm behind the stove. Maria could have stayed in the tub for hours, but she didn't know enough about her new mistress to do anything but obey.

She found clean underwear, stockings, four rags, a shapeless black long-sleeved dress, and an apron on her bed. As soon as she was dressed, she went back into the kitchen. Frau Schroeder was at the stove.

"Eat," she said, pointing.

There was a piece of fresh black bread and a bowl of hot stew with small chunks of ham, potatoes, carrots, peas, and onions on the kitchen table. Real food. No sawdust. No bugs. The smell made Maria salivate. It was the first proper meal she'd had since she left home. Slowly, she picked up the spoon, her hand shaking. She lifted the first spoonful to her mouth. She savoured the richness of the gravy, the sweetness of the carrots, and the starchy comfort of potatoes. She chewed slowly. It was just like Aniela's home cooking: simple, hearty, and delicious. For a moment, Maria thought she might cry.

All the time Maria was eating, Frau Schroeder stood at the stove, arms crossed, smoking and watching her. Maria scooped up the last of the gravy with her bread and looked up at Frau Schroeder. She badly wanted more food.

Frau Schroeder read her mind and ladled another spoonful of stew into her bowl. "Don't expect this every day. You'll earn your food from now on, but I want you strong enough to work, not fainting from hunger."

Maria thanked her. When Maria was finished eating, Frau Schroeder sat down opposite her. "Dr. Schroeder and I have no children, so your work here will be easier than in most houses."

Maria looked at her and realized that, under the artfully applied makeup, Frau Schroeder was not a young woman.

"You will give me all your food stamps," continued Frau Schroeder. "And I will give you food every day. You will have half a Sunday—four hours—of free time every other week. And—this is important—you will never, never go outside this house without your OST badge. Understood?"

Maria nodded. As Frau Schroeder outlined Maria's duties, Maria had a hard time focusing on what she was saying. The travel, the warm bath, the nourishing meal, and the stress of the last few weeks were taking their toll. She was exhausted. But as Maria listened, it slowly dawned on her that as long as she performed her chores well, she could go out. She could write to her parents. She could receive packages in the mail. She hadn't expected any of this after the way she had been treated in the brick factory and the transit camp.

One of the first things Maria did was write to her parents, telling them she was all right. Like everything else, the postal system was in chaos, so she didn't get a reply from Aniela and Sergei until later that summer.

On July 27, 1943, Aniela wrote: *Starting today, I will concentrate on you exclusively. I have to wash the lining of the overcoat and sew it back on, and I have to remake the velvet dress and also some underwear, and all this will have to be sent to you. I have a new fashion magazine for 1943 from Berlin; there are such wonderful cuts there, and I'll make a velvet dress for you based on that new magazine.*

Aniela ended happily: *Be healthy and happy to my greater joy, take care of yourself. Covering you with kisses: your little eyes, little nose, little mouth, your hair and your little callused hands. Loving you, your mama. Dad too is kissing you.*

Then, on August 26, 1943, another letter arrived, this time from Sergei: *Write to us whether we should send you a toothbrush, tooth-brushing powder, cologne. I implore you to write to us about everything.*

Cologne, powder, just like she had at home! This was wonderful. And there was more. Sergei ended his letter with a plea: *We implore you not to be cast down by anything, to endure submissively everything, and, with God's help, you will, alive and well, come back home to us. We kiss you innumerable times. Your loving dad and mama.*

Sergei understood Maria. She was their miracle, their golden daughter, so she had been spoiled and protected. At times, she was wilful, stubborn, unforgiving. She had a temper. And she had no life skills.

But neither Sergei nor Aniela understood that the Maria they were writing to was not the same Maria snatched by the Nazis. For this new Maria, Würzburg represented a type of freedom. She was out from under her parents' control for the first time.

Maria thought a job as a housemaid for a couple of years wouldn't be so bad.

Chapter 6

Chance Encounters

At 8 Schillerstrasse, Maria quickly learned to cook and clean, becoming the perfect housemaid. She understood that her food and benefits were dependent on the whims of Dr. Schroeder and his wife. Initially, she was careful, obeying their rules.

She was fascinated by Frau Schroeder, a cool, pragmatic beauty who ran the house like a military operation. Frau Schroeder had fed Maria well the first day because she wanted to build her strength. No point having a housemaid who could faint at any minute. But after that, Maria's food was strictly rationed.

Maria was always hungry. As she grew more comfortable in her job, she plotted how to steal food. Her favourite trick was to wait until the Schroeders were both out. Then she would cut a slice from the loaf of dark rye bread. She would take the slice and the loaf to the balcony. While she ate the slice, she would point the loaf at the sun. Soon a thin crust formed, disguising the cut. Sometimes Maria smeared a thin coat of sweet butter on her slice. She never got caught.

She was always on her best behaviour when Dr. Schroeder was home. The doctor was a handsome, heavy-set man over six feet tall. His light-brown hair was combed back, revealing a high forehead, his eyes were pale grey, and his mouth was always set in a slight frown. He said he was an ear, nose, and throat specialist, yet he and his wife had this beautiful, large apartment for just the two of them. And they had a housemaid, a perk bestowed by the Nazis on party members in good standing who were useful to the Third Reich. Maria never found out what Dr. Schroeder did that was so important to the Nazis.

Maria didn't think about the Schroeders too much. She hadn't seen Lena and Valya for two weeks now and missed them terribly, but she was in teen heaven—no parents, no school. Ironically, because she was an Ostarbeiter and it was wartime, she was relatively free. She relished her four hours off every second Sunday.

Her first Sunday off, she walked to Ring Park, a couple of blocks from 8 Schillerstrasse. She hated wearing her OST badge and took to covering it casually with a scarf if few people, soldiers, or police were around. The park was peaceful, full of gravel paths winding through towering trees, topiary bushes, shrubs laden with buds, flower beds with the first signs of spring peeking through the dark earth. The sun was shining that first Sunday. The park smelled like spring.

Maria strolled along a track, her shoes crunching on the gravel. A red squirrel scurried across her path. She turned to look at it as it disappeared into the shrubs. When she turned back, an attractive young man was walking toward her, hands in his trouser pockets, shoulders hunched, wearing an old sports jacket and a scarf tossed casually around his neck. Strands of his wavy brown hair kept falling in his brown eyes. He was slim and about six feet tall.

Maria was lowering her gaze, about to pass him, when she saw the OST on his jacket. He noticed hers too. They both stopped and looked at their badges.

"When did you get here?" he asked.

"Just a few minutes ago," Maria replied.

He smiled. "No, I meant, when did you get to Würzburg?"

"Oh," said Maria, blushing. "About two weeks ago."

"Ah. Where are you from?"

"Vinnystia. And you?"

"Odessa. We're practically neighbours."

"How long have you been here?"

He grunted. "Too long to care anymore. I'm Nikolaus Kobetz," he said and thrust out his hand. "I work at the Robert Unkel soap factory across the river."

"Maria Brik. Nice to meet you. I work for Dr. Schroeder and his wife."

They stood, considering each other.

"Look, I'm going to meet some friends, just like us," Nikolaus said, looking pointedly at her OST badge. "Would you like to come?"

Maria hesitated. She had never been alone with a strange man before. She could see he was older than her, but not by much. She bit her lower lip, considering what to do. She liked his sad brown eyes.

"Don't worry," Nikolaus said. "Nobody will hurt you. A group of us from home meet up in the park when we can. It's just good to be with our own people and get away from all this madness." He smiled sadly. "Even if only for a few hours."

Maria nodded and followed Nikolaus. He guided her expertly along paths to a clearing where a small group of young people sat on benches and at the fountain's edge, chatting and laughing. They were all wearing OST badges, but here, in this peaceful park, they could forget, for a few hours, that they were slaves in a foreign land.

As Nikolaus led her to a seat, she heard, "Maria! Maria! Maria!"

Maria turned. There, running toward her, were Valya and Lena.

Maria had given up hope of ever seeing Valya and Lena again. But there they were, at the fountain in Ring Park. The girls couldn't stop weeping and hugging each other.

Nikolaus sat on a bench in the sunshine, listening to the excited chatter. He watched Maria. There was something in her manner and her innocence that attracted him. Her joy at seeing her friends made him smile.

"Look," said Valya, fishing out a small package wrapped in paper from her coat pocket. She unwrapped it carefully, revealing pieces of Linzer cookies. Maria and Lena gasped. Even in pieces, the buttery sandwich cookies were mouth-wateringly beautiful.

"They dropped on the floor in the bakery, so they couldn't sell them. The owner said I could have them this time because I'm such a good worker. I saved them for us. I knew we'd find each other."

Valya handed Maria and Lena a bit of cookie each. The girls ate slowly, letting their tongues roll around the jammy bits.

"I think it's strawberry," said Maria, closing her eyes, focusing on the flavours. "Yes, definitely strawberry."

Suddenly, Maria was sad. The little shard of cookie reminded her of all the treats Aniela and Sergei had given her. Would she ever see her parents again?

Lena interrupted her thoughts. "I don't get any cookies, but I'm not treated too badly. The family I work for has a big department store. They have two other girls from Ukraine at the house. We all get along, but I'm the last one, so I get all the dirty jobs. You know, cleaning toilets, washing the floor, and doing laundry. God, there's so much laundry!" Lena showed them her rough red hands.

"Well, what do you expect?" said Valya. "They own a department store. Must be nice to have all those fashionable clothes, though." She looked at the relatively new coat and dress Lena's employer had given her. They were castoffs but still better than anything Lena had ever owned in Ukraine. She still wore Maria's hat, though. Her hair was growing in slowly.

Valya looked down at the worn coat her employer had

given her. It was too old, too big, with too many patches to even begin to look fashionable, but it was warm. "Ladies, I give you the finest German outerwear." Valya opened her coat and twirled.

Maria and Lena laughed.

"May I bring your attention to this very special decoration, brought to you compliments of the Third Reich." Valya grinned, pointing to the OST badge pinned to her coat. Then she started goose-stepping with her right arm thrust out. "Heil Hitler!"

Maria and Lena stopped laughing. Nikolaus leaped off the bench and put his arm around Valya, forcing her arm down. "Never, never do that again," he warned. "You don't know who may be watching. You could get yourself and your friends into very big trouble. Assume everyone is a spy."

"Are *you* a spy?" giggled Valya.

"Luckily for you, I'm not." Nikolaus looked around. People had stopped talking and were looking at them. Then, somewhere, a bird chirped, and people started talking again.

"I'm sorry," sighed Valya. "It's just sometimes I can't take this anymore. They're all monsters. What have we ever done to deserve this? I just want to go home." She began weeping.

Lena took her in her arms. "It's going to be all right," she soothed. "Don't worry—"

"It's war," interrupted Nikolaus. "You were in the wrong place at the wrong time. All of us were. Now we're all paying the price. Thou art a slave! Don't you get it? You have no freedom. Of course we all get frustrated, and in our frustration we can make a stupid mistake, like you just did. So what will that get you? Huh? An early death, that's what. If you don't want to die, don't do anything stupid. It's that simple! We don't know when or how this madness will stop, but this war will end. Let's see who wins. Then we'll act." Nikolaus turned and walked back to the bench.

Valya looked at him, and then turned to Maria. "Who was that?"

"I really don't know. I just met him today in the park. He's from Odessa and works at a soap factory across the river. But he's right, Valya. We all have to be so careful. I don't want anything to happen to you or Lena. You're all I have in this insane place. And we've just found each other again." Maria hugged Valya and Lena hard.

When the girls broke apart, Maria joined Nikolaus on the bench. "I'm sorry for what my friend did. We're new here, and I guess we don't know very much."

Nikolaus studied her. Then he smiled. "It's all right. You'll learn. But keep an eye on that one." He tilted his chin toward Valya.

Maria nodded. "I have to go now."

"When's your next day off?"

"Two Sundays from today."

"I'll be here at the fountain."

Maria smiled and returned to Valya and Lena.

"Well?" said Valya, looking back at Nikolaus.

"He wants to meet me here next time."

"He's good-looking," said Lena.

Valya frowned. "We'll walk you back so we can see where you live," she said. "Let's figure out a way to keep in touch so we can meet again."

Valya linked arms with Maria and Lena. As the girls walked, they filled each other in on their lives since they had arrived in Würzburg.

AFTER THAT, MARIA'S LIFE took on a new purpose. She worked hard, and Frau Schroeder was more than satisfied. Maria also found that sharing her parcels from home with the Schroeders earned her more perks: She had more food; she could go out more often. She and Valya and Lena started exploring the city in their time off. It was always wonderful being together. Best of all, no one knew what they were doing. At least, that's what Maria thought—until she received a letter from her mother in which Aniela admonished:

Musya, today, Valya's mama called in and she mentioned that Valya wrote to her that, on a day off, you two went somewhere for a stroll in a forest, 10 kilometres outside the city, on a tramway, and that a policeman approached you and ordered you to get off the tram.

Musya, I beg you very, very much—do not get angry with me for saying this to you—why should you look for embarrassment, ride a tramway, only to be kicked off, and in general, why go 10 km away from the city into a forest? In my view, you girls indulge yourselves too much, and thereby you expose yourselves to all sorts of dangers.

Maria was angry with Valya for blabbing to her mother about their adventure. It was none of Aniela's business what she did in Würzburg. Hadn't Aniela abandoned her to this fate? She had no right to tell Maria how to live her life.

Maria became angrier still after she read the rest of Aniela's letter:

You must not forget that you are girls, and that you are in a foreign land. Nobody will spare you, and therefore you have to spare yourselves. It is better to stay on the balcony at home, even though it's not your true home, but still, home it is. Better stay there than venture out so far away. Where to, why, and to what purpose? Don't forget, either, that it's wartime now.

But Maria had forgotten about the war. As Sergei and Aniela continued to scold her through their letters, Maria became more defiant. She considered herself a woman. She didn't need her parents.

She saw Nikolaus regularly. Often, they went to a quiet area of the park. He would kiss her face, her mouth, her hands. More often now, he would caress her breasts, and his hand always travelled to the secret spot between her legs. She would strain against his hand, impatient for more caresses. She loved him. Yes, she loved Nikolaus. And she was certain he loved her too.

Then, one Sunday when she went to their meeting place, he wasn't there. Maria waited, but Nikolaus never showed up.

"Where's Nikolaus?" she asked one of his friends.

"They moved him somewhere else. I don't know where. He's gone from Würzburg."

Gone? Maria couldn't believe what she had heard. She sat, dejected, on one of the benches beside the fountain and stared down at her hands. Eventually, Valya found her. Maria told her what had happened.

"Don't worry, he'll write to you. I'm sure he loves you. Just wait a bit, until he gets settled."

Maria never got a letter from Nikolaus. Instead, it was Sergei who wrote on October 19, 1943:

We came across Madam Fastykovskaya. She said that she had received a letter from Valya, where she says that your acquaintances had left for other destinations. Musen'ka! I believe you to be a sufficiently lucid girl, and that you can assess the situation perfectly well, in that one should not maintain a correspondence with people that you know too little about. Please take this well into consideration, and in general, please correspond only with us and your girlfriends.

Maria resented Valya and her big mouth. Couldn't she find something else to talk about in her letters home? Did she always have to tell her parents what she and Lena were doing? Didn't Valya know her big-mouth mother would tell Aniela everything?

Maria's world in Würzburg had become so comfortable, she could indulge in this petty squabble with Valya. Maria refused to think of, or speak about, the technicum, the brick factory, the ordeal in the cattle cars, or the Wolfstein Transit Camp. She blocked everything from her mind and lived in the moment.

She forgot it was wartime.

Chapter 7

Barracks, Ball Bearings, and Bombs

Maria ran as fast as she could. She could barely breathe. Her heart was hammering. The explosion had rattled every cell of her body. She stopped. She was lost, confused by the clouds of dust, the smoke, and the noise.

"Maria! Maria!" Olga materialized through the veil of dust and smoke and grabbed Maria's hand. "Run! Run, Maria!" She dragged Maria farther away from the factory.

"Here! Here!" screamed Olga. She pushed Maria into a shallow trench, nothing more than a depression in the ground. Olga and Maria held each other as the world blew up around them. The girls tried to press themselves into the bottom of the trench as explosion followed explosion.

The noise stopped first. It took longer for the dust to settle and the smoke to dissipate. Finally, Maria and Olga climbed cautiously out of their hole. Maria was crying.

"It's okay," comforted Olga. "This was your first

bombing. You haven't even been here a week. Shh, shh, I know it was really scary. It will be easier next time, I promise you."

Maria stopped crying and looked at her. Next time? She saw other workers emerging from similar depressions in the ground like zombies, brushing dirt from their clothes.

"Welcome to Schweinfurt." Maria recognized the woman wiping dirt from her mouth. They shared the same barracks. "You get your very own personal bunker here," she said, pointing to the ground. "The Nazis were kind enough to let us dig them ourselves. Isn't that nice?"

Germany was losing the war. The Nazis had moved all slave labourers to essential industries to support the Wehrmacht. No more housemaids for loyal Nazis like the Schroeders. Maria had been sent here, to Schweinfurt, the ball-bearing capital of Germany.

Only Nazis were allowed in the underground bunkers at the factories. Slave workers had to shelter in shallow holes in the ground they dug themselves. According to the Nazis, they were all *untermensch*—subhuman. And all subhumans were disposable. The SS guards had been told to work them to death.

"Back to work!" An SS guard hit Olga. "Your American friends bombed the shit out of the river. What idiots! The factory is safe, so get back to work. Now!"

The girls made their way back to their stations on the assembly line. In Schweinfurt, Maria had a grim daily routine: roll call at 4 a.m. outside the barracks, no matter the weather; weak, bitter fake coffee for breakfast; and a 3-kilometre march to the Kugelfischer factory, where she stood for twelve hours making ball bearings. Lunch was thin soup with vegetable peelings, the vegetables often unwashed. Or just fake coffee. Sometimes they had a piece of bread bulked up with sawdust. Minutes later, it was back to work. At the end of a long day, everyone marched back to their barracks for another meal of watery soup and stale bread, roll call, and lights out by 9 p.m., when the barracks were locked for the night.

Bombings could interrupt this routine at any time. Each bombing added more work to the daily routine because on Sundays, instead of working in the factories, or what remained of them, the slave workers had a twelve-hour shift cleaning up the rubble and debris. They wore wooden shackles that left their legs sore and bleeding.

Maria remembered her first night in the women's barracks. When she had finally collapsed into her bunk, she could feel the bugs crawling in her straw mattress, and her blanket smelled of the previous occupant. She closed her eyes. She wished Lena and Valya were there. What had happened to them? Maria's tears wet her straw mattress. The bugs stirred.

Apart from the factory, the only other place Maria went was to the toilet barracks. The guards marched the women there in the mornings and evenings. The toilet bowls were in a row, so close to each other that when she sat, she could touch the woman's knee on either side. No partitions, no doors, no toilet paper, no toilet seats. Many of the toilets were smeared with excrement. The smell was nauseating. Yet there was always a lineup—too few toilets, too many women. Maria learned to do her business quickly or the guards would give her a whack.

If the women had to relieve themselves during the night, there was a bucket by the locked door of the barracks. It filled up quickly, and the smell dominated the dank structure.

To the left of the toilets was the washing area. Two large troughs—the kind cattle drank from—ran along the centre of the room. A pipe running above the troughs had faucets. The water was filthy. There was no soap, no towels, no showers. But there was a can of gasoline for washing the lice from your hair with gas—if you hadn't already been shaved bald.

Maria had made a friend in the barracks. Olga came from a small farming village outside Odessa. She was a pretty girl, only sixteen when she was taken. She reminded Maria of Lena. Olga and Maria worked side by side. They were forbidden to talk, forbidden to stop working, but they managed to whisper to each other occasionally. They walked together, arm in arm, to and from the factory, finding comfort in being close.

One day, an SS guard stopped at Olga's station and barked something at her. Olga flinched. She didn't speak German, but she felt the threat in his voice. As the guard was leaving, she turned slightly to Maria and whispered, "What did he say?"

"You'll have to work faster, or he'll beat you."

The guard swung around, heading straight for Maria. He whacked her shoulders with his club. "How dare you speak? No talking at work!" he screamed. "I'll see to it you never break the rules again." He dragged her away and pushed her into a small room. "Twenty-four hours solitary confinement. No food! No water!"

Maria noted a small pot for excrement in the far corner. No bed, no chair, no room to lie down. The guard stared at her from the doorway, then he turned and slammed the door, plunging the room into darkness. There were no windows. Maria felt along the walls. There was no light switch.

About halfway through her confinement, Maria was sitting on the floor, leaning against a wall, when she heard a sound she knew and dreaded. Planes. The drone got louder. She stood up as the first bomb landed. The walls shook. Maria felt frantically for the door. When she found it, she screamed. She pounded with her fists and her shoulders. She kicked it. Nobody came. Her screams were drowned out by the bombs.

They kept falling. Maria's cell shook. She curled into the fetal position, covering her ears, sobbing, expecting to die. Thirty hours later, hours after the bombing had stopped, Maria still lay in the fetal position, wide-eyed, staring blankly into the darkness. That's how the SS guard found her when he opened the door. Light and fresh air flooded the cell.

"*Steh auf! Geh raus!*" *Get up! Get out!*

Maria didn't move. The guard kicked her. Still Maria

didn't move. He closed the door, came back with a bucket of water, and threw it over her. Maria groaned. She blinked, staring at the guard. He kicked her again. Slowly, she uncurled. She got on all fours, then stood unsteadily, using the wall for balance. She was cold and stiff, and she had peed herself. She looked uncomprehendingly at the guard. He motioned for her to leave, escorting her back to her workstation.

Maria walked slowly, mechanically. Her spirit seemed to have been drained from her body, but her mind was churning. The reality of the war, the cruelty of the Nazis, the uncertainty of her future had awakened something deep inside her. She would beat these Nazis by living. She would do whatever she needed to save herself.

In Würzburg, she had been a child. In Schweinfurt, she became a woman. And she became a survivor.

Chapter 8

Freedom

March 27, 1945

The rumour mill at the Kugelfischer factory and in the slave worker camps was in overdrive. It was a whispered hope: *The Americans are coming. The Americans are going to save us. The Americans are winning the war.*

Maria and the others stood at their workstations, their hands automatically feeding the conveyer belts, but their eyes were darting about the factory floor, and their hearts were pounding. No one knew anything for sure, but they knew something big was about to happen.

And it did.

One by one, the Nazi guards melted away from their posts. Soon there were no guards. There was no supervision. One by one, the slave workers stopped what they were doing. One by one, the machines stopped. The factory became unusually still.

The workers looked around, still worried a guard would

leap out of the shadows and beat them. They looked at each other, wondering if their eyes were deceiving them. Were the guards really gone, or was this a trick that would end with more cruelty?

A minute ticked by, and then another, and then the factory erupted. Workers who had endured weeks, months, even years of repression, humiliation, and hard labour scrambled for every exit. There was only one thing on their minds: food. Everyone was starving.

The women stormed the storeroom, Maria and Olga with them. They watched as one woman came out hugging a large sack of flour to her belly. Another woman sliced the bag open with a kitchen knife and flour poured to the ground. Women ate the flour raw, fighting each other for handfuls. The weaker ones were on all fours, licking flour from the ground.

Off to the right of the storeroom, Maria and Olga heard screams. Some of the women had surrounded a Nazi guard who had been helping himself to the food before fleeing. They were beating him with pots and pans. They stabbed him with kitchen knives. One woman had a butcher's cleaver. Her face dripped with his blood. Long after he was dead, the women continued to vent their fury on his body.

Soon there was no food left in the storerooms. No water, either. The slave workers moved to the fields, foraging for mushrooms, root vegetables, dandelion leaves—anything to check their gnawing hunger.

Their only consolation was that, finally, they could go

into the underground bomb shelter at the factory. The Allies were still bombing Schweinfurt, and Maria and Olga could hear the pounding of artillery fire and the roar of planes daily.

April 7, 1945
IT WAS A WARM spring day. Maria and Olga were foraging in the field near the camp, but they found nothing.

"Listen," said Maria, cocking her ear to the sky. "Planes."

They stood still. The drone of planes got louder, accompanied by artillery fire. It sounded close. The girls ran for the bomb shelter and squeezed in among some of the male slave workers.

"I think it's going to be bad," said a man.

"How do you know?" asked Maria.

"Look at the ceiling. It's really shaking badly this time. And the noise is louder."

Maria sighed deeply. Olga sat down on the ground and brought her knees to her chest. She rocked herself, moaning softly. Maria sat with her.

"I'm Viktor," said the man.

"Maria. This is Olga."

The noise got louder. The next explosion sounded like it was just above them. Olga screamed. Dust dropped from the ceiling. People began coughing. With every explosion, more dust. People covered their mouths and closed their eyes, coughing and choking. Olga buried her face in her skirt, and Maria pulled her sweater over her face. Viktor took a dirty rag out of his pocket and tied it over his nose and mouth. They waited in the dark.

Finally, the explosions stopped. No one moved. They sat for about an hour before people ventured outside, slowly and cautiously. Maria, Olga, and Viktor stood by the entrance to the bomb shelter and stared. The Kugelfischer's five-storey administration building no longer existed. Only part of the front facade stood.

"I told you this was going to be bad," said Viktor, shaking his head.

Maria nodded numbly.

"Look," said Viktor, pointing to a huge Nazi flag flying over the tall chimney that was still standing. "That's why we're such a damn good target." He looked around, then added, "I bet this raid hit the train station. There might be food there. It's about a kilometre away. Do you want to go and see?"

"Why not?" sighed Maria. "Starve here or starve there. What difference does it make?"

"I don't want to go," pleaded Olga. "I'll wait here, down below. Please come back for me, Maria."

"No, Olga, I can't leave you. Come with us."

"No! I don't want to!" wailed Olga.

"Leave her be," said Viktor. "We don't have much daylight left."

"Okay, Olga," said Maria. "Stay down below. I will come back for you."

Maria and Viktor picked their way past smouldering ruins and around the rims of craters ripped into the earth by bombs. Maria saw a woman navigating through the rubble with a mattress on her head. *At least she has a place to sleep,* thought Maria.

Many of the buildings still standing had white pillowcases or sheets hanging from windows. Maria pointed to a large white sheet and said, "Does that mean the war is over?"

"Probably. The rats are leaving the sinking ship." Viktor laughed bitterly. "And you know what they say? The bigger the white flag, the bigger the Nazi. All damn cowards." He spat on the ground.

They came to what was left of the train station. The track lay twisted and bent, boxcars turned on their sides or flipped upside down. Maria and Viktor joined the people crawling into the boxcars, searching among broken boards. They found cans of meat and tin tubs of honey. They took as much as they could carry and headed back to the bomb shelter. They were almost there when they came upon a small group of SS soldiers.

"Halt," ordered the officer. He pointed his pistol at Maria and Viktor, who stood perfectly still. Maria took a cautious step toward the officer. Her heart was pounding, but she was going to protect her food, no matter what.

"Herr Commandant," Maria began, politely but firmly. "We are workers from the Kugelfischer factory. We have had no food for days now. We got these at the train station, and now we are going back to the factory to work."

Maria never stopped looking at the commander. A trickle of cold sweat ran down her back. Viktor tensed beside her.

Without a word, the officer lowered his gun, turned to his men, and ordered them to continue marching. Maria started to shake.

"You've got guts," Viktor said, looking at her in admiration.

When they reached the bomb shelter, Olga threw herself into Maria's arms. "I didn't think you'd come back."

Maria patted Olga's back as Viktor opened a can of meat with a screwdriver and hammer. A strong rancid odour filled the air.

"Rotten," muttered Viktor, as he threw the can away. Of the eight cans of meat, only one was good. They divided it up and wolfed it down, barely chewing.

They were luckier with the tubs of honey, scooping up the golden syrup with their fingers. Maria closed her eyes. She was transported to her kitchen table at home, swinging her legs and licking a spoonful of honey, Aniela beaming at her as she dried the dishes. Maria opened her eyes. No! That was before. She had to focus now on staying alive.

Eat and live, Maria.

April 10, 1945

MARIA, OLGA, AND VIKTOR slept with honey-filled stomachs in the bomb shelter. Each day, they went to either the train station or an empty building, looking for food. There was still honey in the train wreck.

That morning, they tried to reach the train station

again. As they walked, Maria stepped on a piece of paper. Bending down to pick it up, she saw it was the front page of the *Schweinfurter Zeitung* newspaper. The headline boasted, "Surrender?—No! We Are Choking with Hate."

Maria, now fairly fluent in German, read on: "Every house must become a fortress that is held or buries its defenders under its wall." Every German, continued the article, was expected "to crack open a tank and kill at least ten enemy soldiers."

Maria threw the paper away. They picked their way into a street that wasn't totally filled with rubble. A few badly damaged houses teetered nearby. A boy emerged from behind one of them. He looked to be no more than fourteen years old. His blond hair covered in dust and dirt, he glared at them through narrowed blue eyes. He wore the uniform of the Hitler Youth and carried a rifle almost bigger than he was.

"Halt or I'll shoot," he said, his falsetto voice confirming his youth. For a brief moment, nobody moved.

"Put the gun away, boy," said Viktor.

"We're workers from the Kugelfischer factory," said Maria soothingly. "You know the Kugelfischer factory? It makes ball bearings for the war."

"Quiet! I am part of the Fuhrer's Werwolf youth! I obey only Herr Hitler! My orders are to kill all enemies of the Reich, like you."

"But we work for the Reich," said Maria, smiling. "You don't have to kill us. Anyway, the war is almost over."

"No! The war will never be over until all swine like you are dead!" he shouted, his face flushed, the rifle shaking in his hands.

Viktor was taking a step toward him when a burst of artillery fire went off nearby. The boy turned around. Viktor leaped forward and wrestled the rifle away. The boy fell to the ground, and Viktor pointed the rifle at him.

"Viktor, no! He's just a boy!" shouted Maria above the cracking of artillery.

Viktor was breathing heavily. "Go!" he shouted.

The boy got up and ran. Viktor checked the rifle. Empty. He threw it after the fleeing boy. There was another round of artillery fire, this time louder, closer.

"Sounds like the Americans are clearing the town, street by street!" shouted Viktor over the noise.

"We have to get back to the shelter!" yelled Maria.

They ran, often stumbling and sometimes falling, back to the bomb shelter. Once they were inside, it sounded like the fighting was directly above them. And then silence. Viktor peeked out from the shelter. It was dark and, for the first time in days, it was completely quiet.

April 11, 1945

MARIA OPENED HER EYES. She didn't know what time it was, but some light was seeping around the bomb shelter door. Olga's head was in Maria's lap. Viktor was snoring beside her. Slowly, people were waking up.

The door to the bomb shelter burst open. In the entry,

the silhouette of a soldier was outlined by the light. Maria could make out his gun.

"*Deutsche soldat?*" demanded the soldier in broken German.

"*Nein! Nein!*" came the panicked shouts from the shelter.

"We are the American Army," announced the soldier. "We have liberated Schweinfurt! You're free."

There was a stunned silence—and then bedlam. People began cheering, hugging each other, and crying. As Maria, Olga, and Viktor emerged from the bomb shelter, they saw thirty or more American soldiers. Maria just stared, not moving.

The soldiers began handing out chocolate, chewing gum, and army rations. A soldier put a bar of chocolate in Maria's hand. She looked at it without speaking. She raised her eyes and grabbed the soldier's sleeve.

"*Danke,*" she whispered, tears in her eyes.

Suddenly, she had to sit. The enormity of what had just happened overwhelmed her. All around her, people were hugging the soldiers, shaking their hands, hugging each other, crying, and eating their precious American treats.

Was the war really over? No more starving, no more beatings, no more disgusting gruel, no more forced marches from the camp to the factory? No more Maria the Ostarbeiter, the slave worker?

She was free. But what did that mean? The Maria who had studied at the technicum and wanted to be a pharmacist was long gone. Who was she now? Where was she to go?

Chapter 9

A Man You Can Trust

Maria woke up slowly. She couldn't lift her head. The light seared her brain. She looked around. *Ach*, she realized, *I'm back in the barracks*. Olga was lying on her side to her right. Viktor was snoring on her left.

It had been two days—or was it just one?—since the Americans had come into their bomb shelter. Maria tried to think, but her head hurt. Her stomach lurched. She crawled over Viktor and ran outside. Bending over, she vomited, then spat, trying to rid herself of the sour taste. Leaning against the door frame, she squinted into the April sunshine.

She remembered the celebrations after they had come out of the bomb shelter. Everyone was wild with joy, while she sat stunned, observing from a pile of rubble. One of the slave workers had pulled her up and danced her around the ruins of the factory. Another one had pressed a bottle of homemade hooch to her mouth while his other hand reached for her breast. Maria had broken away.

Olga ran toward her. "You don't need this anymore," she cried, as she ripped the OST badge from Maria's chest. "Come on, we're going to celebrate!"

Maria joined a large group as they ran into Schweinfurt, stumbling over rocks and rubble. They broke into stores, helping themselves to food and liquor. They ate and drank and danced. They marched into abandoned homes. There was a piano in one of them. Someone climbed on it and stomped on the keyboard with his wooden clogs.

They were drunk with freedom. Everything they had endured, all the demeaning, barbaric acts, were wiped out. They were free from rules. Free from Nazis. Free from their own consciences. Freedom was a shock, like a dam bursting, unleashing the power of humanity at its best, and its worst. Emotions spilled out uncontrollably as the world went on a liberation bender, the party fuelled by plundered booze or homemade hooch.

The survivors danced. They cried. They made love, hungry for the human warmth denied them for so many years. They also raped, robbed, and murdered. An eye for an eye. Let's get those German bastards who did this to us. The party was a grotesque carnival, releasing what had been repressed even before the Nazis got to them.

Maria had drunk from a bottle being passed hand to hand. But when someone said, "Let's go and find some Nazi scum and kill them," a warning light went off in her head. She hid as the group went hunting.

Maria had wandered aimlessly among the ruins. She couldn't believe the destruction. She couldn't believe how one angry little man called Adolf Hitler could destroy so much. How could anyone follow him and help him tear apart families, homes, and countries? She had never believed in God. This was proof to Maria there wasn't one.

As it started to get dark, Maria had looked around for Olga, for Viktor. Somehow, she had lost them. She stumbled over some rocks.

A hand reached out to steady her. "Hey, sweetheart. I've got you."

Maria saw a man dressed in ragged clothes teetering toward her out of the debris. He was breathing hard, and he stank of alcohol. Gripping her arm, he slurred, "Hey, come on. Let's have a little fun."

"Let me go."

"Not until we have a little fun, sweetheart."

He dragged her closer. He was strong. He reached his other hand up her dress. Maria screamed, but there was no one to hear her. She managed to jerk herself free and fell backward, landing hard on the dirt and debris. The drunk fell on top of her.

As they struggled, Maria felt a rock beneath her hand. She pounded it into his head. The man screamed. Maria gathered all her strength and pushed him off. Then she ran. Finally, she stopped, panting in a doorway.

When she had her breath back, she looked around. Where was she? She could see a fire in the distance. People were singing, dancing, and laughing. Maria crept closer to get a better look.

"Olga! Viktor!" she shouted, and broke into a run.

Olga detached herself from the partiers and staggered into Maria's arms. "Maria, where've you been?" Olga hugged her tightly, almost losing her balance.

"I don't know. I got lost."

"Maria! Maria! We found you," shouted Viktor, coming toward them. He pushed a bottle of schnapps into Maria's hand.

Olga and Viktor would take care of her. She lifted the bottle and forgot all her troubles.

Now, hours later, Maria sat by the entrance to the barracks, staring into space. Olga stumbled out, clutching a bottle of schnapps, and offered it to Maria. She took a drink. It helped. The two women sat together in the warm sun.

"Maria, look." Olga pointed to two figures approaching.

Maria shaded her eyes. They came closer, and she could see they were Americans, their liberators.

"Hello, ladies. Everyone okay here?" asked one of the soldiers as he knelt down beside them.

Maria and Olga shook their heads.

"All right. Well, we've got a truck just down the road. Let's get you to the assembly centre. We've got clean beds, clothes, food, and medicine. Looks like you two need a little help."

"Can we take our friend Viktor too?" asked Maria.

"Yes, ma'am. Where is he?"

Maria pointed inside the barracks.

As the first soldier went looking for Viktor, the other

soldier gently took the bottle of schnapps out of Maria's hand and replaced it with a container of water. He gave one to Olga too. After Viktor emerged from the barracks, the soldiers led them to a truck with other slave workers sitting in the back.

"All right, everyone, we're off to the assembly centre. You're going to be safe there. We're gonna find out who you are, and then we'll help you go home. Okay, everyone?"

People nodded.

Olga squeezed Maria's arm. "Oh, Maria, can you believe we lived to see this day? We didn't die. Sometimes I really thought I wouldn't make it. I couldn't take one more day at that factory. I thought the war would never end."

"Yeah, I did too. I almost feel like this is a dream and if I wake up, I'll be back in the factory again."

"No, no, Maria. You're never going back there again. Never! You're alive, Maria. You can do whatever you want. Oh God, I'm so happy."

"Me too," said Maria, hugging Olga.

"What are you going to do now?" asked Olga.

"I don't know. Get some food. Wash."

"I want to go home. I want to see my mother and my father and my brothers. I hope they're all still alive. Are you excited about going home, Maria?"

"No." Maria looked away. "I'm not going home."

Olga pulled away. "What? Why not? Don't you want to see your mama and papa?"

"Yes, I'd like to see them. But Mama always said to me, 'If you ever get a chance to leave Ukraine, take it. Go!

Don't come back. Papa and I will be fine. Go and build a new life. Get away from these Communist bastards. Get away from the fascists. They're all monsters. You'll never have a future here.'"

"But you have to go back. That's what the Americans said."

"I don't care what they said. I'm not going back."

"But, Maria, if I go back and you don't, we may never see each other again."

"Olga, I just can't go back."

"But then, what are you going to do?"

"I'll figure something out."

The truck drove between stark twenty-foot-high pillars that framed the entrance to the assembly centre. A sign on the right pillar said *Panzer Kaserne*. Maria and Olga looked in dismay at the German eagle and swastika glaring down at them from a corner of the first building.

When the truck stopped, Maria counted ten large buildings, four to five storeys high, sitting in neat rows along a main street. Some had gaping holes in their roofs; one was reduced to its foundations. Pretty well all had rubble piled outside. Maria and Olga looked at each other. They were expected to stay here?

"Sorry about the mess," said a GI approaching with a clipboard. "This used to be a German military base, but our flyboys kind of messed it up." The soldier chuckled. "But there are plenty of buildings that are still good. And it sure beats the heck out of where you've been staying for the last few years, right?"

A few people nodded.

"Okay, let's get you to your rooms. The mess hall is that building, and if you want some clean clothes, Private Gillespie will help you over there. Once you're settled, go to that small office there." The soldier pointed to a building with a large line of displaced persons—DPs—winding from its front door into the street. "That's where you get registered, and then we'll help you go home. Sound good?"

Nobody said anything. It had been years since they were asked their opinion.

"But first things first." The soldier smiled. "A little dusting. Before you can go anywhere in the centre, we're gonna spray you with a little DDT powder, okay?"

People looked at each other, confused. DDT? Dusting? Like what the Nazis did to them? Many looked at the soldier with fear.

"Don't worry, it's harmless," continued the soldier. "We've all been sprayed. DDT will make sure you don't have any bugs. You don't want to catch typhus, do you?"

A soldier approached Maria with a round metal cylinder attached to a compressor. There was a long nozzle at one end of the cylinder. He poked the nozzle under her skirt, up the sleeves of her dress, in between her breasts, and through her hair, releasing fine DDT powder into every nook and cranny. Maria cringed in embarrassment. Dusting, she later found out, took place every month at the assembly centre. And every month Maria—and most of the camp—did their best to avoid it.

Maria turned to Olga. "Oh God, that was horrible.

Let's get some clean clothes before we go to our room. I can't stand these rags anymore."

They found the clothing building and Private Gillespie.

"What are you looking for?" he asked.

"Anything clean. And some shoes, please."

The soldier left and returned with a printed flower dress, a fine grey wool skirt, a cotton short-sleeved pale-blue blouse, and two pairs of brown leather shoes. "I got two pairs of shoes in case one doesn't fit. And here—" He tossed a second blouse at Maria. It was long-sleeved yellow silk. "I thought you'd look good in this." He smiled.

Maria held the silky blouse to her shoulders. The fabric was slippery and cool. For a moment, she remembered some of the beautiful fabrics Aniela had for her clients. Maria shook the thought from her head. She held the other clothes to her body. They seemed like they would fit, and both pairs of shoes fit.

"We don't do returns, so if they don't fit, trade them with somebody else," Private Gillespie said, and then he outfitted Olga.

Maria and Olga clutched their clothes to their chests as they looked for their room. Their building seemed to be relatively intact. They went down a long, wide hallway with twelve doors on either side. Their room was large, with two windows, two steel bunk beds, four wooden cabinets, a table, and four chairs. The space was simple and clean.

Maria put her clothes on a bed and found the toilets at the end of the hall, a communal bathroom with six concrete sinks on one side with faucets and mirrors above them, six sinks on the other side, and two long, wide benches in the middle.

Maria walked in and stopped abruptly. There was someone staring at her. She put her hand to her mouth. The person did the same thing. She lowered her hand to her throat. The person copied her.

It took Maria a full minute to realize she was looking in a mirror. She hadn't seen herself since she left Würzburg. Who was this emaciated person staring back at her? Her cheeks were sunken, her hair hung in dirty, greasy strands, and her soiled, torn dress hung off a skeletal body. And her breasts. Where were her breasts? She lifted her hands to her face. Her nails were ragged and filthy. She wanted to crumble to the floor and cry.

But she was done with crying. There was still running water in the bathroom. She stripped, dumped all her clothes into a garbage can, and walked into the large shower room. The retreating Nazis had left some soap. Maria turned on one of the faucets and stepped into the warm water. She held her hands over her head. Slowly, she danced under the water.

Olga found her, and she stripped too. They laughed and danced, rinsing away the grime of the Kugelfischer factory and the camp.

OVER THE NEXT FEW weeks, the assembly centre filled with former slave workers from other factories and farms around Schweinfurt. POWs, Polish soldiers, and Resistance fighters came too. Thousands of displaced people, with more pouring in every day. The assembly centre was becoming a booming, overcrowded small town.

It took the Americans, and the newly arrived team from the United Nations, a while to process everyone. There were so many people in the assembly centre, Maria was able to dodge getting processed immediately.

People could go into town at will. Maria overheard snippets of conversations among the DPs.

"Look. Swiss-made!" A DP was pointing to a watch hanging loosely on his thin wrist. "Got it from a German—for just a few cigarettes."

"I went into a bakery and helped myself to everything. Nobody stopped me. And if they'd tried, here's what they'd get." The DP, his face twisted in hate, held up his fist.

Maria and Olga's roommate, Tanya, bragged about her adventures in Schweinfurt. "Look," she said, laying silk stockings across her bunk. "I got these, and extra chocolate too. From one of the GIs. You just have to do them little favours." She winked. "There's more where these came from. I can help you get some."

"No, thank you," said Maria.

Olga shook her head.

"Suit yourselves, girls," said Tanya. "You know, this is a man's world. You're not gonna get far without a man. You've gotta play the game."

Maria had no intention of "playing the game." She had everything she needed, for the moment. But she couldn't avoid registration much longer.

The next day, she ran into Viktor.

"How are you doing?" asked Viktor.

"Okay."

"Have you been processed yet?"

"No. You?"

"Yeah. I told them I wouldn't go back to Poland because it was captured by the Communists. I don't want to live in a Communist country. I wouldn't go back no matter how much money they offered me. I want to go to Australia."

"Australia?"

"Yeah. I've had it with being cold. I'm waiting to get papers. How about you? Tell me you're not going back to Ukraine. The word is that Stalin's insane. The minute you get back, you'll be treated like a traitor. Stalin says you should have died for your country instead of coming home. Doesn't matter if you were a POW or abducted. Bastard! He's sending people to special camps up north to get 're-educated.' Just be careful. Stalin's agents are everywhere, trying to convince people to go back."

"I don't want to go back, Viktor. But I don't know what to do."

"You speak Polish, right?"

"Yeah."

"So tell them you're Polish. You lost all your papers and you don't want to go to Poland because it's going to be a Communist country. Tell them you want to go to Australia like me. Hey, come with me!"

"And they'll believe me?" asked Maria, avoiding the invitation.

"Are you kidding? Nobody has any papers. They're so busy, they'll believe anything you tell them. They just want to get you out of their hair as fast as possible. It's worth the risk."

"Viktor, my friend!" someone shouted behind him. "How's the application for Australia going?"

The voice belonged to a Polish soldier. The two men embraced, thumped each other on the back, and laughed.

"Maria, I'd like you to meet my friend Stanisław Żebrowski. Stan's from the same part of Poland as me. We're practically neighbours." Viktor gave Stanisław another slap on the back.

Maria stared into hooded brown eyes and offered her hand. Stanisław held it for a second, gently flipped it over, and kissed the top lightly. He smiled sadly, never taking his eyes off her.

Maria withdrew her hand slowly. *Handsome*, she thought, *with good manners*. He had dark-brown hair under his soldier's cap, a straight nose, a full lower lip, and a high forehead. He wore a shabby Polish soldier's uniform, obviously not his, as the jacket was too short, but it was clean. He was not tall, under six feet. He exuded sadness and a world-weariness barely covered up by his good manners.

He must have seen and done some terrible things in the war, Maria thought. She suspected he was older than her, yet she was overcome by a need to hold him and comfort him.

"I'm trying to get Maria to go with me to Australia,"

joked Viktor. He told Stan about his idea that Maria should pose as a Pole.

"Your Polish sounds pretty good," said Stan.

"Thank you," murmured Maria. She felt shy, too aware of her shapeless dress. Her hair was clean, and she had gained some weight, yet she felt unattractive, like a clumsy schoolgirl, in Stan's presence.

"Good! That's a start. I got processed yesterday, and I'm waiting to go to Canada. Bigger than Australia." Stan smiled at Viktor. "Lots of work there too. Would you like to come to Canada, Maria?"

"I don't know. I just don't want to go back to Ukraine."

"And that's very smart of you. Why don't you let me help you? I know the questions they'll ask you. I could help you with your Polish too, and then you won't have to worry about anything."

"You'd do that for me?"

"Anything for a fellow Polak." Stan winked.

"All right."

"Are you doing anything right now?"

"No."

"Good. Let's get started. We'll need a notebook, and I know exactly where to get one."

He hooked Maria's arm under his. "See you later, Viktor."

Viktor shook his head and laughed. "Well, well, well, Stanisław Żebrowski and Maria. Who would have thought?"

Maria smiled as Stan led her away. Stan reminded her of her father. He looked like a man she could trust.

Chapter 10

Beginnings and Endings

Maria was in love. For two days, Stan had been tutoring her for her DP registration at the assembly centre in Schweinfurt. Maria had to force herself to pay attention as she wrote in the notebook Stan had given her. Being near Stan was a big distraction.

Maria wore the yellow silk blouse Private Gillespie had given her and styled her hair with Olga's help, the two of them giggling like the schoolgirls they had been before their nightmare with the Nazis.

"The first thing you have to decide," Stan advised, "is your last name. Your first name, Maria, is fine. In fact, it's a beautiful name." Stan paused. "Just like the owner." He smiled. She lowered her eyes. "But Brik will give you away because it isn't a typical Polish last name."

"My mother is Polish. I could take her maiden name, Kotecka."

"That's perfect. Now, where was she born?"

"Rowno."

"Good. That's where you were born from now on. Okay, the next two questions are important. First, why did you come to Germany?"

"I had to."

"No. Say 'I was forcibly taken away by the Germans.' Write that down and don't forget it. They'll also ask you if you want to go back to Poland."

"Of course not. I've never been there."

"Just say no. Then they're going to ask you, 'Why don't you want to go back?' So you say—and write this down—'I do not agree with the current political regime in Poland.' Okay?"

Maria copied everything into her notebook.

"So now they're going to ask, 'Have you ever been persecuted by the Germans because of race?'"

"I'm not sure what that means."

"It doesn't matter. Just say, 'Yes, because I am a Pole, and the Germans wanted to exterminate our race.' Okay?"

Maria nodded and kept writing. "But some of these are lies. What if they find out?"

"They won't. Remember—you lost all your papers. Trust me. They're way too busy to worry about one pretty girl. Just do what I tell you and you'll be all right."

Maria nodded and closed her notebook.

Stan put his hand over hers. "It'll be okay, Maria. You need to get your DP registration to stay here or go to any of the other camps. Now go join the line and get registered while everything is fresh in your head. Come see me when you're done. I want to see your ID card." Stan smiled. "I'll be around my building over there."

Maria started to leave.

"Maria, wait! Give me your notebook. You don't want them to think you've been cheating." Stan chuckled.

Maria joined the line of DPs at the registration desk. Before she knew it, she was standing in front of a young GI about her age. He still had pimples. He yawned. He ran through his list of questions through an interpreter without even looking at her. Maria answered exactly as Stan had coached her.

Ten minutes later, Maria had a stamped ID card. She looked at it in wonder. She was now Maria Kotecka from Rowno, Poland. She was also a Catholic. Religion had never been discussed or practised at home. She would have to remember the details of her new identity from now on. She hurried to show Stan her ID.

As she rounded the corner to his building, she stopped. Stan was leaning against the wall in conversation with a pretty young woman. They were laughing. Stan gave the woman a hug. Maria's enthusiasm ebbed away. She was turning to leave when Stan noticed her.

"Maria!" he shouted. "How did it go?"

Maria drew herself up and walked to him and his companion. "It was easy. I just came to show you my ID and to thank you for all your help."

"Didn't I tell you it would be easy?"

"Yes, you were right. Thank you again." Maria turned to leave again.

"Hey, wait a minute. I want you to meet Janina. She and her fiancé, Henryk, are Polish. Janina, meet my friend Maria."

"Oh," said Maria in a small voice, as she felt the tension leave her body.

Janina extended her hand to Maria. "Stan told me about you. Congratulations on getting your ID. Where are you from in Poland?"

"Rowno," lied Maria. "I'm pleased to meet you too."

Maria looked at Stan for approval. They were speaking Polish, a language Maria had spoken only at home with Aniela. She wondered whether her Polish was good enough to fool Janina. Stan nodded and smiled.

"Janina and Henryk were in the same labour camp when they were liberated," Stan said. "Then they came here. We met a few days ago. Hey, where is Henryk?"

"Oh, you know Henryk." Janina laughed. "Probably trying to find some eggs."

"Eggs?" asked Maria.

"Yeah, eggs. We always tease him about eggs. In our labour camp, the men were divided from the women by a big fence. So one day I was walking along the fence with a bunch of women, and this guy from the other side yells, 'Hey, anyone here from Łódź?' I yelled back, 'I am!' And so we met. Then we kept meeting at the fence, and Henryk started smuggling eggs across to me, one at a time. So we hatched a romance." Janina laughed. "All it took was some eggs and a fence, and now we're engaged."

"Well, go find Henryk," said Stan. "We've got to celebrate Maria's victory. And tell him to bring his eggs."

THAT NIGHT, MARIA, STAN, Janina, and Henryk found some chipped glasses, and Stan got a bottle of homemade schnapps. Olga and Viktor joined them.

"Here's to Maria, a brave Polak!" Stan winked and threw back his schnapps. He kept refilling the glasses until Maria lost count.

Olga pulled her aside. "Oh, Maria, you did it. I'm so happy for you."

"Thank you. You know, I was so worried, but Stan really helped me."

Olga looked at Stan, who was singing a Polish folk song. "Mały biały domek" was a sad song about a small white house where the singer was once happy with his beloved, but now she was gone, and he was left with only the memories. As Stan sang, he waved his glass in time to the music and swayed, but he never took his eyes off Maria.

"I don't want to spoil your party, Maria," whispered Olga, "but I'm leaving tomorrow."

"What? Where are you going?"

"I'm being transferred to the Soviet sector. And then they'll help me go home."

"No, no, don't go." Maria grabbed Olga and held her. "Stalin's crazy. You'll be sent to some other camp up north, probably to Siberia, for 're-education'! Don't trust the

Soviets. They'll treat you as badly as the Nazis did. Olga, they're calling us collaborators. They don't trust us. It's going to be bad for you there. And there's no guarantee you'll ever see your parents. Please don't go, Olga."

"Maria, you know I have to. I know it's risky, but I have to take a chance. I miss my mama and papa so much." Olga was crying now.

Viktor gave Olga a hug and patted Maria on the back.

Stan walked toward them, wagging his finger. "Hey, Viktor, my friend. No touching my girl. No, no, no."

Stan pulled Maria away from the group and started singing again, dancing Maria around the room. She forgot about Olga. All she could think about was Stan calling her "my girl."

The next day, Olga left. Viktor was leaving too, for another Polish DP camp to wait for his immigration papers for Australia. It was a bittersweet parting for the three friends. Despite all the bravado, all the suppressed tears, all the promises to see each other again soon, the three knew, deep in their hearts, this would be their last moment together.

Viktor struggled to hold back his tears and keep his voice steady. "Ah, Maria, Olga, the war brought us together, and now peace is tearing us apart. What a crazy world." He held the women tight.

Maria wept. She was remembering another parting—from Valya and Lena. But they had never gotten to say goodbye. Yes, she cried for Olga and Viktor, but mostly she cried for herself. Everyone she loved was torn from her by this stupid war. Her parents, Valya, Lena, and now Viktor and Olga.

Maria saw them off and then trudged back to her room, heartbroken and hungover. Janina found her curled up in her bed. She sat down next to her and took her hand.

"Maria," said Janina softly. "How are you?"

"Terrible. I miss Olga."

"I know, but Olga followed her heart. You have to follow yours."

Maria buried her head in her pillow.

Janina sighed. "I know how hard it is. I'm not going back. Ever. I love my family, Maria, but there's no future in Poland. You have to be brave now. You're going to have an exciting new life in a new country. Trust in the future, your future."

"But I'm all alone."

"No, you're not. You have me and Henryk. And Stan. He likes you. We'll go through this together. Polish solidarity, right? Hey, we might even wind up in the same country. Besides, didn't you hear the latest announcement?"

"No."

"They're moving all us Poles together to another camp. We're leaving in a few days."

"All the Poles?"

"Yes. They want people of the same nationality together in one camp. Less fighting that way." Janina paused. "I think it's a good idea. So we're going to move, Maria."

Chapter 11

The Khaki Labyrinth

Maria stared in disbelief at the ramshackle wooden barracks. This was where she was going to live? She turned to Stan. They had become lovers in Schweinfurt.

"Stan—" she began.

He stopped her. "Don't start, Maria. It'll be okay. At least we're in the same barracks. I told them you're my fiancée."

"Really?" Maria placed her hands on her hips, cocked her head to one side, and smiled at him.

"Yes, really. Now come on. Let's register and get our beds before everything is gone."

Maria sighed and followed Stan. He was all she had left now. Could he fill the crater left in her heart? Could she rely on him? He was eleven years older than her. Would that be a problem?

The La Guardia DP camp in Weiden had fifty-eight barracks. More communal living. It would be worse than the assembly centre in Schweinfurt, where she had shared a room with only Olga and Tanya. Now, she and Stan would be moving into a barracks with God knows how many others. Maria's heart sank as she and Stan were assigned to number thirty-two, along with ten women and thirty-six men. Janina and Henryk had married in Schweinfurt and were in a different barracks with families. Janina was pregnant.

The camp was run by the United Nations Relief and Rehabilitation Administration (UNRRA), which decreed that every barracks had to have a leader reporting to them. Stan was elected *barakowy*—leader of barracks 32. Maria wasn't surprised. Stan had been a soldier—an *uhlan*, part of an elite Polish light cavalry unit. He had a natural air of authority.

Well, at least that's something, thought Maria. She was looking forward to the perks his leadership would give them. Stan would be responsible for the distribution of UN and Red Cross rations.

But first things first—they needed to set up some kind of home in barracks 32. UNRAA issued them khaki-coloured blankets, sheets, and pillows. Stan moved two beds with straw mattresses together in a corner.

"Look, Stan." Maria pointed to their roommates. "They're building walls around their beds with suitcases. And look over there, they're hanging blankets as walls to give them privacy. Can we do that?"

"Yeah, sure. I'll get some rope and some extra blankets." Stan winked, eager to test his authority as *barakowy*.

Before long, Maria had a double bed, a small table, two chairs, and three empty suitcases that served as a chest of drawers inside her khaki domain. She was protected from the prying eyes, but not the eager ears, of other residents of the khaki labyrinth. When the barracks was organized, there was corridor of khaki blankets and stacked suitcases running its length. It looked like an apartment hallway. At one end, there was a wood-burning stove and some basic pots and pans, if anyone wanted to cook, but most ate in the kitchen barracks. There was also a toilet block. The setup wasn't great, but Maria accepted it. She was sure she and Stan wouldn't be there long.

She was wrong.

A few days after their arrival, Stan came into their curtained cubicle, took off his Polish army uniform, and put on civilian clothes.

"What are you doing?" asked Maria. She was lying on the bed, looking at an American movie magazine.

"Obeying the law," grunted Stan, as he pulled up the new trousers. "UNRAA says no more uniforms."

"You can't wear your uniform?"

"Nope. But it's better that way. I can blend in when I go to town."

"Town? What for?"

"You'll see. Where did you get that magazine?"

"A guy from UNRAA gave it to me."

"What guy? When?"

"I don't know. Just a guy. A few days ago, when I was visiting Janina."

Stan looked at her. He was about to say something, thought better of it, and walked out.

Barracks 32 started getting fresh meat, fruit, and vegetables as Stan illegally traded UNRAA and Red Cross rations with the Germans in town. In the winter, he quietly organized equally illegal raids on farms. Barracks 32 always had enough wood for their stove and fresh food for their bellies. Maria, of course, benefited the most.

Stan had just returned from Weiden after bartering with a baker for some pastries, the ones Maria loved—though Stan was learning fast that Maria loved all pastries.

"Stan, I have something to tell you," Maria whispered, mindful of the others in the barracks. "Sit down beside me." Maria patted the bed. "I'm pregnant, Stan."

She waited anxiously for a reaction. Stan didn't move. He didn't say anything. He just stared at her. Maria looked away and bit her lower lip.

Finally, Stan reached for her hand. "Maria, my beautiful Madonna, I'm so happy. We will have to get married, of course."

Maria expelled the breath she had been holding and embraced Stan. She knew he would take care of her and the baby. She had been impressed with the way he handled himself as *barakowy*. She knew he had earned his leadership skills and smarts not just from the Polish army but also from his time in a prisoner of war camp. In Schweinfurt, Maria had asked him what he did during the war.

"Oh, you know, I fought," Stan answered. "I was part of the Polish cavalry."

"Did you fight on horseback?"

Stan laughed. "No. Horses are no match for Panzer tanks. Horses have their uses, like spying on enemy lines, but not against tanks. We fought on foot, just like the regular infantry."

"When?"

"When the Nazis invaded Poland in 1939. At the Battle of Sochaczew. It was in September, just when the war started. The Germans were stronger and we lost. I was captured."

"Captured?"

"Yeah." Stan looked away. He seemed to be lost in thought. He hung his head and clasped his hands. "The truth is, I sat out the war in the Nazis' finest stalags," he said wryly.

"Oh," said Maria softly. "What was it like living in the stalag?"

"It was no picnic, that's for sure. The last stalag I was in was IV-B in Mühlberg. Have you heard of it?"

"No."

"It was bad. The worst of all the stalags, I'm telling you. Thirty thousand prisoners. Overcrowding, disease, bad living conditions, terrible sanitation, no clothes. In the winter, it was freezing. I wore rags on my head and stuffed rags and papers in my boots to keep my feet warm. Shit, people were dying all the time from typhus and malnutrition. There was hardly any food. You had to be really smart to get something to eat."

"What?" interjected Maria. "Don't they have to feed you?"

"Oh yeah, the Germans fed us all right—crap bread, mouldy potatoes, scraps of cheese, some processed meat, and phony coffee. It barely kept us alive. We all waited for the Red Cross parcels. That's what kept us going."

"You survived," said Maria, as she unclasped his hands and squeezed one.

"I guess I survived. Here I am with a beautiful, smart woman who's very curious." Stan kissed Maria's hand and looked away quickly.

But Maria wasn't finished. "What were the barracks like?"

"Well, you know, barracks are barracks. They were just like this one. Shitty wooden shacks, just enough room to cram everyone in. We Poles were all together. We had triple bunks and straw mattresses. Oh God!" Stan's voice rose. "The bugs and the lice. And we only got to shower once every three months!" He looked past Maria.

"They'd line us up and march us into town—Mühlberg—to the public showers. And while we showered, they fumigated our clothes. We put on the same stinking clothes, only now they were full of powdered poison. Ah, Maria." Stan released a long sigh. "I really don't know how I survived. Five and a half years of my life—gone."

Stan lowered his head. He looked at their clasped hands. *I'm not going to cry*, he promised himself. That part of his life was done. He looked at Maria. Yes, he had a future now, with his beautiful Madonna.

"How did you escape?" she asked.

"Well, the commandant of stalag IV-B was a guy called

Markus König. He used to be a teacher. He was reasonable, not cruel like some of those bastards. He knew the war was just about over. So a few days before the Russians came, he called a meeting of the leaders of the different nationalities in the camp. He called these guys 'his men of confidence.'"

Maria leaned in, listening intently as Stan talked about the last days of his years as a prisoner.

"König told them Germany had lost the war. No one was surprised—word was getting around. König said the Soviets were on their way and these 'men of confidence' had to look after their own nationalities. He said if the prisoners wanted to leave, the German guards wouldn't stop them. So a lot of us left. The ones that stayed had to face the Russian Cossacks on horseback, then the NKVD. The secret police were worse than the Cossacks. I heard later it was very bad for the Ukrainians and Poles who stayed behind. Very bad. The Russians were as cruel as the Nazis. Actually, worse. They hated us more."

Maria put her arms around Stan. He sagged into her embrace and kept talking, wanting to get his story out. "I didn't want to stay anywhere near the Russians or the Russian zone. I wanted to get into the American zone, but first I had to cross the Elbe and, Maria, it's one hell of a wide river. There was a bridge about 15 kilometres away, so I hid during the day, and at night I stole food wherever I could and just kept walking and walking. I thought my legs would give out. I was so hungry when I left that damn stalag. I don't know where I got the energy, but I kept going. I swore I would never let those damn Russians get me. When I saw the bridge, I had to figure out how to get across, so I hid and waited. There were Russian patrols roaming around and Waffen SS goons who didn't believe the war was over. It wasn't safe to cross the bridge, so I hid again, but that night I started creeping along the bank, and I got real lucky, Maria. I found a small boat and rowed across. Finally, just when I thought I couldn't take one more step, I saw the American flag. I almost cried. I was in the American sector. They fed me and took me to Schweinfurt. And to you." Stan's shoulders heaved gently as he buried his tears in Maria's embrace.

"Oh, Stan, you're safe now, my darling. We have all we need here, and we have each other." She pulled Stan into a long kiss.

Maria was happy. She was going to have Stan's baby, and they were going to get married. Everything was great, except for one little thing that kept niggling at her. What would her parents say about the coming marriage, the baby, and her lies on her ID card? Maria decided she wouldn't tell them anything right now. How could she write them? The war had just ended, she reasoned. The postal system was barely operational. Aniela and Sergei were probably busy rebuilding their lives. Best to wait for things to settle first.

ONE DAY, AFTER MARIA and Stan had been in the La Guardia DP camp for two weeks, Stan was walking back to the barracks when a young Polish man called out, "Hey, are you the *barakowy* for 32?"

Stan looked at the man. He was younger than him and holding four large fish. "Yeah, I'm Stanisław Żebrowski. Nice fish."

"Nice and fresh. I just caught them today. I'm Frank Użarowski. Maybe you want some fresh fish for dinner tonight?"

"Maybe. How much?"

"Ach, nothing. Take them all. Maybe later I might need something. Okay?"

Stan looked at Frank. He liked his style. Stan extended his hand. "Okay."

Frank handed over the fish.

"Were you in the army?" Stan asked.

"Nah, I was too young. But I joined the Home Army. I was a marksman. You?"

"Yeah, I was in the army. Lancer. I got captured. Spent the war in three POW camps."

"Wow! The whole war?"

"Yeah, not much fun."

"Well, I got captured by the Germans too. Smuggling Jews out of Poland. I escaped. Then I got captured by the Russians. And I escaped again. Then I got captured by the Americans for crossing two borders!" Frank laughed as if it were all a big joke. "So here I am. But not for long."

"Where are you going?" asked Stan.

"Canada. Just waiting for my papers. Good country. Lots of fish. And hunting too."

"Yeah, the more I hear about Canada, the better it sounds," said Stan. "Maybe we'll meet there, you never know. Hey, come over to 32 and have a drink and meet my girl."

They found Maria sunning herself on the bench outside the barracks. Her eyes were closed, the top two buttons of her blouse were open, and her skirt was pulled up to her thighs.

"Maria, look who I met."

Maria opened her eyes. The sun silhouetted the man. She shaded her eyes with her hand, and her blouse moved a bit farther down her chest.

"This is Frank Użarowski, and look what he gave us for dinner."

Maria didn't notice the fish. All she saw was wavy brown hair, a loose curl hanging down a high forehead, broad shoulders, and a sweet, boyish smile. She smiled.

"Maria, fix yourself," said Stan, pulling her skirt down.

Maria stood up and shook Frank's hand. She and Frank locked eyes. Maria couldn't breathe. Her heart beat wildly.

"Maria, here," Stan said, shoving the fish into her hands. "Cook these. Come on, my friend, stay for dinner."

Frank followed Maria into the khaki labyrinth.

Chapter 12

Warning Signs

"Maria, let's get married as soon as possible," urged Stan.

Maria hadn't expected this. She had told Stan she was pregnant two weeks earlier. He had mentioned marriage, but Maria felt he was talking about a wedding sometime in the future. Not now.

Maria narrowed her eyes. She was wary, given what had happened last night. Frank had showed up with fresh fish again, so Stan invited him to stay for dinner. During the meal, Frank had entertained them with his war stories. Maria was delighted, and she thought Stan was enjoying himself, but after Frank left, Stan had slapped her hard across the face.

"Whore! I saw the way you looked at him! You better stop it or else …"

"Or else, what?" Maria yelled back.

She touched her cheek. It hurt. She glared at Stan.

The khaki labyrinth had suddenly become quiet. Maria felt everyone holding their breath. The *barakowy* and his girlfriend were fighting. She had walked out and sat on the bench outside, replaying the night's events. Stan had never behaved this way before. Yes, he had been drinking. Given what he had been through, he often drank. But he had never hit her before. Maria was furious. Why shouldn't she have looked at Frank? At least he was fun.

At dinner, they had learned Frank was eight years younger than Stan. He had grown up on a farm close to Stan's family farm in Nienalty, in northeastern Poland, close to the Russian–Polish border. He loved fishing and hunting. Stan nodded approvingly. He loved the outdoor life too.

Frank told them how, when the Germans invaded Poland, a friend had asked him to take a family of Jews across the border to Russia to safety.

"I was only seventeen, but I knew the woods. Even in the dark," Frank explained. "So, all in all, yeah, I helped about 150 Jews escape."

"Ever hear about the Battle of Sochaczew?" interrupted Stan.

"Yeah, sure. Everyone knows about that."

"Well, I was twenty-five when I went to fight," said Stan. "Just three weeks into the war, and bang, they got me! Five fucking years in those damn German stalags. The whole war! I was a prisoner, but you know what? Surviving in those stinking hellholes was almost as bad as—no, I think worse than—fighting. And I did it." Stan emptied his glass and banged it on the table.

"I was captured too," Frank countered. "And tortured."

Maria's eyes widened. "Did it hurt?" she asked.

Stan reached for another drink. He moved his chair closer to Maria and put his arm around her.

"Yeah, but what can you do?" Frank shrugged. "I was helping a Jewish family. Seven of them. It was night. We were in the woods when, all of a sudden, the damn Germans surrounded us. Well, they tortured us real good and locked us up in this old shed for the night."

Maria leaned forward. "Then what happened?"

Stan glared at her.

Frank smiled. "The shed had a dirt floor, so we dug a hole under the wall and escaped." He laughed.

"Lucky you," slurred Stan. "I had to stuff my boots with papers and rags so my toes wouldn't freeze off. And I wore rags under my hat. Tied them under my chin so my ears wouldn't fall off. Ha, I looked like a fucking babushka." Stan poured himself another drink.

"Yeah, that's bad," agreed Frank before returning to his story. "I was captured again, this time by the Soviets. I was in the Resistance. The Soviets didn't like us Poles at all, no sir. They were going to send me to Russia, but I escaped."

Stan grunted. Maria beamed.

"Eventually, I got into the American zone. Then the very first day, I ran into two American soldiers. And son of a bitch, they arrest me! The Americans! What stupid luck."

"Why did they arrest you?" asked Maria.

"I didn't have proper papers. Shit, the Americans and their papers. Almost as bad as the Germans. I had to serve a year in prison. Now, here I am, Buzny at your service." Frank laughed again.

"Buzny?" asked Maria.

"That's me. Buzny was my code name in the Resistance. Buzny at your service, madam." Frank gave Maria a little bow and raised his glass to her.

Stan had had enough. He drained his glass and glared at Frank. *You little boy*, he thought. *Playing games in the woods while real men did the real fighting.*

After Frank left, Stan had stumbled to their cubicle and hit her. Afterward, Maria sat on the bench outside the barracks, fuming. When she had calmed down, she went to bed. Stan was already snoring heavily.

So Stan's question in the morning came as a surprise. After last night, getting married as soon as possible was the last thing she had expected him to say. But he said it. He even begged for her forgiveness. And he promised he would never hit her again. It was just that he loved her so much and he was so afraid of losing her.

Maria forgave him. A voice deep inside warned her to be careful, but she chose to ignore it. She was pregnant. She needed food, money, and a new life in a new country for herself and her baby. Stan was her ticket out. He was talking about taking her and the baby to Canada. So she told Stan she would marry him.

ON MONDAY, NOVEMBER 4, 1946, Stan held Maria's arm as he led her through the archway in the market square in Weiden. Maria was wearing a striped jacket buttoned over a brown woollen dress. A hanky hung jauntily out of the breast pocket. She had brown loafers and white socks on her feet. Her hair was curled and styled in the latest fashion. The jacket cleverly hid her bulging tummy.

Stan wore a Polish army uniform, but he'd had trouble finding one that fit. In the end, he found a jacket that was a bit short but would do. The trousers and cap were a better fit.

The couple posed for a wedding picture. Maria's left arm was bent over her stomach. Stan stood on her left side; his hand slipped under her elbow and held her left wrist. She was his now and he would guide her every step. Stan didn't know that, with Maria, that was impossible.

Maria smiled softly, looking at the camera confidently. She had her man. Stan had only a hint of a smile, his sad eyes shaded by his soldier's cap.

Janina and Henryk came with them. As Maria climbed the stairs to the registrar's office in City Hall, Stan guided her by her arm. She could smell the schnapps on his breath, but she ignored it. The ceremony was short. They walked back through the square, along the Hammerweg Road, to the camp. The sky threatened rain.

That night, barracks 32 threw them a party. Frank came and Stan greeted him with open arms. Why not? He had won. Stan danced and sang till the wee hours of the morning.

Maria didn't drink. She was pregnant and exhausted. She let Janina guide her to bed. She didn't notice when, hours later, two men threw Stan into bed beside her.

The next morning, Maria slipped out of bed. Stan was snoring loudly. She dressed, made herself some coffee, and went to sit outside. Oh God, what had she done?

Maria stopped herself. She had a provider for herself and her unborn child now. Nothing else mattered.

As she grew big that winter, so did the camp. La Guardia expanded with a school, a church, and an infirmary. Everybody was waiting for something to happen. They filled out form after form, seemingly endless miles of paperwork. Each form meant weeks, sometimes months, sometimes years of waiting. The camp was in limbo.

Frank drifted in and out of their lives. There were no more jealous tantrums. Maria spent a lot of time with Janina, who already had her own baby, Jadzia. Maria was terrified of childbirth, and nothing Janina said calmed her.

One day, as she watched Janina change Jadzia's diaper, Maria's water broke. Janina called for help. UNRRA officials guided Maria into the back of a jeep, her eyes wide with fear.

"I'll send Stan to the hospital," shouted Janina as the jeep pulled away.

Maria was taken to the Weiden City Hospital on Bismarckstrasse, a five-minute drive away. There, her labour began in earnest. Stan got there half an hour later. He paced in the waiting room.

Twenty hours later, on Thursday, April 10, 1947, at ten

thirty at night, with the help of a German midwife, Maria gave birth to a baby girl. She and Stan called her Halina Żebrowska because all female surnames in Polish ended with "ska" and the male names with "ski."

Maria knew nothing about babies. Stan knew more, but he was too busy with the duties of being the barracks leader to be much help. Maria relied more and more on Janina.

"Such a sweet baby," cooed Janina, rocking Halina in her arms. "You're lucky. She really is no trouble at all."

"Yeah, you're right. She doesn't cry much. We can actually sleep at night," said Maria. "But she needs so much attention and space. Look at us!" Maria gestured around her khaki-covered corner of the barracks. "We have no room for a baby."

Privately, Maria blamed Stan for Halina. She didn't want any babies. She was too young for that. Stan was older. He should have been more careful.

"But you're not staying here forever." Janina interrupted her thoughts. "You'll all leave soon. I think Henryk and I and little Jadzia are going to America soon."

"Ach, what will I do without you?"

"You'll survive, Maria. You always have."

"I hope so. Stan keeps checking on the paperwork, but nothing's happening."

"Something will happen. You'll get out, Maria. I know it."

A COUPLE OF MONTHS later, Janina's prediction came true. It was a hot July day in the barracks. Maria was flushed and tired. Stan ran in, excited. "Maria! Maria! We're going to Canada."

"Canada?" asked Maria, as she moved Halina to her other breast.

"Yeah, Canada. We're going to Canada!" he exclaimed. "There's this guy in the camp from Canada, and he wants workers. He's interviewing people now. Come on, let's go."

Halina had fallen asleep. Maria cradled her four-month-old infant in her arms as she hurried behind Stan. In front of the La Guardia camp offices was a table with two chairs on each side. On one side sat a middle-aged man in a wrinkled, dirty shirt and trousers, wiping his face with a red handkerchief. His face was as red as his hanky.

George Wilson assessed the couple rushing toward him. The woman with a child in her arms looked healthy. The man was older, but he also looked healthy. The man could handle a long day's manual labour, he thought.

George started unpacking the suitcase that lay on the ground beside him. As he moved his dirty underwear and shirts aside, he sighed. Maybe at this camp he could do some laundry. He reached for the application forms with their three carbon copies, pens, a stamp, and an ink pad. After more rummaging around, he lifted out a small Red Ensign Canada flag on a little base and put it on the table. He lined up his supplies and waited. The camp interpreter slid into the chair beside him.

George knew the routine. He had been to the DP camps in Frankfurt, Feldafing, and Wildflecken. When Ottawa had assigned him to Germany, he barely had time to pack a suitcase with a couple of changes of underwear, three shirts, application forms, and all his office supplies before he was shipped off. Canada was racing other countries to get the best workers the DP camps had to rebuild their postwar economies. The camps offered the world's best one-stop bargain-basement shopping.

George had hitched rides with the Americans or UNRRA officials from camp to camp. Now he sat sweating in the sun at the La Guardia DP camp, wondering how long it would take Ottawa to send proper teams to process the DPs. There was only so much he could do by himself. For one thing, he was running out of application forms.

He motioned for Maria and Stan to sit. There was no small talk. They all knew why they were there. Still, George's first question caught Stan by surprise. Stan asked the interpreter to repeat it.

"Show him your hands," the interpreter said.

Stan held out his hands. George felt them. He hated this part, but Ottawa had insisted. "We're not looking for brains, George," his boss had said. "We want brawn, muscle, young, healthy men. And women. So check their hands for calluses. The more calluses, the more useful they'll be."

An internal memo was more specific: *Any Displaced Person who would be permitted to come, it was assumed, would be selected like good beef cattle with a preference for strong young men who would do manual labour and would not be encumbered by aging relatives.* It was signed *John Holmes, First Secretary, Canadian High Commission, London, England, 1947.*

George told Stan and Maria their application was acceptable, but there were still more tests, more forms to fill out—a medical exam, fingerprinting, and inquiries with the camp police. Maria was worried. Would her lies hold up? Stan didn't seem concerned. He asked where he and Maria would go in Canada.

George looked at him. "Canada thinks you'll do well in the logging industry. We're a big country. We need lots of help clearing our land."

Stan brightened up. "Where in Canada?"

"Probably up in northern Ontario, a town called Timmins. You'll love it there. Lots of Polish DPs like you and your wife. Good fishing and hunting too."

Maria said nothing. She was thinking about Frank. He was still coming around since Halina was born. Maybe they'd meet in Canada, she thought.

Stan and Maria shook George's hand. As they prepared to leave, George said, "Remember, it's going to take time, but we'll get you to Canada."

Neither Stan nor Maria understood how long it would take to leave Germany. There was more paperwork, mountains of it—health inspections, criminal checks from the La Guardia police, immunizations, and passport photos. By the time the paperwork was completed, the Żebrowski family had been moved to a new camp to continue waiting. The whole process took about four years.

But that was in the future. Right then, Maria had a task she could no longer put off. She had to write to her parents. The last time she had written was five years ago, from Würzburg. She felt guilty, and she knew Aniela and Sergei must be distraught, wondering if she was alive.

She had a lot to tell them—she was in a DP camp in Weiden, she was married, she had a daughter, Halina, and she was emigrating to Canada. The reply from Vinnytsia was swift.

Aniela, now sixty-five, wrote, *I cry no longer now; I enjoy my happiness, that you are alive and well and that, more than that, God has sent me wonderful little Halinochka.*

Aniela wrote that Sergei was so overjoyed he bought Halina a pair of little socks, knowing she would never wear them. Aniela said he would take them out of the drawer and hold them.

Maria folded up the letter slowly. She had promised she would continue writing to her parents. But it was a promise she would find difficult to keep.

Chapter 13

Camp Hope

Maria sighed happily as she, Stan, and Halina entered the front gates of Camp Tikvah. Even the menacing German eagle at the entrance couldn't suppress her high spirits. Maria saw rows of buildings in good condition; well-dressed, happy people; and a fairy-tale mountain towering over everything. Best of all, no barbed wire surrounded this camp as there had been in the La Guardia DP camp.

La Guardia had closed down in June 1949. Camps were closing as DPs either went home or to a new country or to another camp to wait for immigration papers. She wasn't surprised when she, Stan, and Halina were transferred to a camp in Bad Reichenhall to wait to go to Canada. The camp was already a sanctuary for Jewish concentration camp survivors, and they had named it Tikvah—"hope" in Hebrew.

UNRRA officials assigned them a room in one of the

buildings—a real room with four walls, two beds, and a door. Privacy at last. They were also given another bed for Halina and two cupboards, two chairs, one stove, one stool, and two tables. For Maria, this was unprecedented luxury. They would have to return everything when they left, but for now, it was theirs. Maria put Halina on the floor to play while she set about making their room a home with some housewares and bedding she had brought from Weiden.

Stan went to talk to the camp administrators about their immigration status. As soon as he left, Maria got her purse. From a slit she had made in the lining, she took out a photograph she had hidden there.

The photo was taken in Weiden at Christmas in 1947. It showed her with ten-month-old Halina in her lap, Stan on her right, and Frank on her left. They were all sitting in front of a Christmas tree. The men stared straight ahead. Frank, his face expressionless, had his arm casually thrown behind Maria's chair. Stan had the barest hint of a smile, his body turned to Maria but his eyes staring at the camera, almost as though he were saying *See them? They're not fooling me. I know what's going on.*

Between the two men sat the golden daughter, Stan's Madonna. Radiant. Beautiful. Smug. The prize both men wanted. Maria stared confidently at the camera with a hint of a smile.

From the minute they met, Maria knew she was falling in love with Frank. She had tried to deny it, but Frank woke feelings in her she had never known before. A deep hunger for him permeated every cell of her body. She wanted him. But she was pragmatic. She wore a mask of studied indifference every time she saw Frank, especially if Stan was around.

Frank had always found a way to see her. Usually he brought fresh fish and stayed for dinner. Or they would all eat together in the dining hall. After Stan had a few drinks, Frank risked looking boldly at Maria, his hunger for her clear on his face. Sometimes he squeezed her hand under the table.

As she sat in her new room at Camp Hope, Maria ran her finger over Frank's face in the photo and smiled. She remembered his boyish, lopsided grin, his eternal optimism, and his passionate eyes. She remembered the fish dinners. She had gotten good at cooking fish. Her smile faded. Could she dare hope they would somehow be together again?

She thought back to the day in La Guardia when Frank had announced he was leaving. It was on Halina's first birthday, April 10, 1948. Frank had arrived at their barracks unexpectedly, without any fish.

"Here." Frank gave Maria a small package wrapped in newspaper. "For Halina."

"Not fish, I hope." Maria laughed. "Halina still doesn't have teeth."

It was a small rattle. Halina grabbed it happily.

"I have some news," Frank said. "I'm going to Canada."

Maria's heart stopped. "When?"

"I'll leave Weiden in June."

Stan, who was sitting at the table watching Halina, stood up. "Did you see that George Wilson guy?"

"Yeah."

"Well, how come you're going now? He told us we'd have to wait a year or more. He said not to hold my breath."

"I don't know, but I think it's because I have no dependents, and they want miners. I have some experience."

"Where are they sending you?"

"Timmins, somewhere up north in Canada."

"Hey, I'm supposed to go to Timmins too."

"Timmins, Ontario?"

"Yeah. I'm supposed to be working in logging. I think a pulp and paper place."

"I'm going to work in a gold mine. They're going to give me some training."

"Well, well, aren't you the lucky one?"

"I guess. Hey, I can help you when you get there."

"Sure, Frank, that would be great. Maria and I would love that. Let's celebrate. To Timmins! To Canada! And to lots of money!"

Suddenly, Stan felt magnanimous. They were getting out of this German hellhole. Sure, he was suspicious about Frank and Maria, but he could control her. He'd let Frank show him the ropes in Timmins, and once his work term of two years for the Canadian government was done, he and Maria would move somewhere else in Canada, without Frank. Yeah, the future was looking bright.

Maria had felt Frank's eyes on her as Stan went to the dresser to fetch the homemade schnapps. She picked up Halina and hid her face behind her daughter's head. *Timmins!* she thought. She and Frank would be going to the same place in Canada.

Just before he left La Guardia, Frank had followed Maria to the camp store. While Maria was looking at the canned goods, he stood casually beside her, pretending to be interested in cans of Spam.

"Maria," he whispered.

Maria stiffened and moved Halina to her hip closest to Frank as a buffer. She kept her eyes and free hand moving along the rows of cans.

"Maria, I love you. I will wait for you in Timmins. Okay? I will! No matter how long it takes, I will wait for you."

Maria nodded numbly, blinking back tears. "I love you too, Frank," she whispered to the cans.

In their room at Camp Hope, Maria heard footsteps coming down the hall. She tucked the picture back in its hiding place in her purse. She still smarted from the slap in Weiden. Maria tried not to trigger Stan, but sometimes she would smile at some man, knowing Stan would see. She couldn't help herself. She wanted to hurt him, but not too much. She still needed him to get her to Canada. She was buoyed with confidence, knowing she would soon be meeting Frank in Timmins.

AFTER THEY HAD BEEN in Camp Tikvah for a year and a half, Stan's immigration approval came through. On December 28, 1950, he left Maria and Halina and headed for the port of Bremerhaven and the ship that would take him to Canada.

Maria had peace at Camp Tikvah. She made friends. If she wanted to walk by the river or stroll to the Café Reber in Bad Reichenhall for a creamy, rich pastry, she had to answer to no one. For the first time, she was free.

Maria had pictures taken of herself and Halina. She sent one to her parents of Halina standing on a tree stump with her dolly. She made sure Halina was well dressed for the fashion-conscious Aniela.

Maria's favourite picture was of herself, caught in mid-stride crossing a street in Bad Reichenhall. Suitcases of stylish clothes had arrived in the camp, and Maria and three friends played dress-up. They curled their hair in the latest style and put on makeup and dark sunglasses, just like the glamorous stars in Hollywood she loved to read about in the American movie magazines she collected. Maria knew the names and lives and loves of all the biggest stars. As she crossed the street, smiling happily, she channelled her favourite—Lana Turner.

Maria forgot the camp, the Nazis, Sergei, Aniela, Stan, Frank, and Halina. She was living her fantasy life, abandoning herself to the fun the war had denied her. There was no one to disapprove.

For one brief moment, she was happy. She was free.

Her carefree days ended four months later when she got her papers to follow Stan. On May 2, 1951, Maria left the camp with four-year-old Halina. She also left behind all hope for the life of her dreams.

She boarded the train for Bremerhaven and the ship that would take them to Canada. Maria was about to start a new life, in a new country, with a man she wished she had never married.

PART II
DECEPTION

Chapter 14

Timmins Triangle

On July 20, 1951, Maria and Halina walked down a gangway linking the *MS Nelly* to Pier 21 in Halifax, Nova Scotia. A volunteer had pinned tags to their sweaters: *Destination Timmins Ontario. To be fed.*

Another damn badge, thought Maria. At least this one didn't brand her as subhuman.

They walked with the other DPs into a room the size of a gymnasium with muddy green walls. Pipes ran along the ceiling; large lamps hung from cords, little beacons of light dotting the room. At the far end, immigration officials sat at long desks, with pens, paper, stamps, and ink pads at the ready. The DPs were ushered to wooden benches facing them. Maria and Halina sat, waiting and watching children running around, mothers hushing crying infants, people coughing and sighing, men shouting to officials and stabbing fingers at their documents, and the elderly, sitting silently, hands in their laps. They had already seen too much, experienced too much. This was nothing they couldn't bear. What was another delay when your whole life had been put on hold?

An immigration official checked Maria and Halina's documents, ticked them off a list, and stamped everything.

"Welcome to Canada," he said, smiling.

Next, their luggage was searched in the Customs Hall. Maria didn't understand what the Customs official was looking for, until she saw what was behind him: A long table sagged under the weight of sausages of all kinds, loaves of breads, wheels of cheese, fresh fruit, homemade wine, honey—the last taste of home many DPs had stuffed in their suitcases. All illegal in Canada. Officials, fearing hoof-and-mouth disease, incinerated everything.

Finally, Maria and Halina made it to their train, across from Pier 21. The steam locomotive trailed smoke as it chugged north to Montreal, Ottawa, North Bay, and, finally, Timmins. The trip took two and a half days.

By the time they arrived, Maria and Halina were exhausted. When the train stopped, Maria told Halina to wait by the door and gave her the blanket they had been given in Camp Hope before they left. The blanket had been the only cover they'd had as they tried to snatch some sleep on the train.

Maria lifted their suitcases off the train one at a time. Then she helped Halina down. She looked around. Finally, she spotted Stan walking toward them. She pointed him out to Halina. Halina tried to hide behind her mother's skirt, suddenly shy at seeing her father after all this time, but Stan picked her up and swung her around. Still holding his daughter, he hugged and kissed Maria. She swayed with fatigue.

"How are you, Maria?"

"Tired. Hungry."

"Okay, let's go home. It's not far," said Stan, putting Halina down and reaching for the suitcases.

"We're going to walk?"

"Sure, Maria. It's only four blocks."

Maria sighed. She just wanted to lie down and cry. Instead, she took Halina's hand and followed Stan. As Stan strode ahead of them, Maria studied her husband. He had gained weight and muscle. He was oblivious to the tired woman and child struggling to keep up with him. Maria wondered if he was still drinking.

Stan led them past a few stores on a main street and then turned onto Birch Street. A few houses in, he turned into a narrow driveway. Maria and Halina followed him into the backyard of a modest wooden house.

"Here we are. Home!" Stan pointed to a staircase leading to the second floor.

"Up there?"

"Come on. It's a great apartment."

Stan scrambled up the stairs with the cases. Maria followed, dragging an increasingly heavy-legged Halina by the hand.

Maria entered a furnished one-bedroom apartment with a kitchen, bathroom, and living room. She barely glanced at the cheap furniture. She wrinkled her nose. The apartment smelled musty.

Maria and Halina cleaned themselves up and joined Stan in the kitchen. He pushed a plate of pierogi and bowls of borscht toward them.

"You cooking now, Stan?"

Stan ignored the jab. "It's from the GV."

"What's the GV? A store?"

"Big hotel in town. All the DPs go there when they arrive. That's where I stayed before I found this place."

Stan opened a bottle of vodka, poured a glass, and offered it to Maria. She shook her head. So he was drinking.

Halina managed to eat some soup, but her eyes were closing and her chin was slowly sinking into her borscht. Stan picked her up and took her to a cot in the bedroom.

Maria followed. She saw the double bed. "I have to sleep," she muttered.

Stan returned to the kitchen. Maria undressed and fell into a deep sleep.

THE NEXT MORNING, she woke with Stan snoring beside her. Halina was sitting up in her cot. Maria took her to the bathroom and then the kitchen. All the food from the night before was still on the table, along with the dirty dishes and a half-empty bottle of vodka. She began clearing the mess. She found milk, bread, cheese, some oranges, jam, and powdered coffee. Halina devoured an orange, juice dripping down her cheeks.

Maria stepped out on the back stairs with her coffee. The yard below was small, enclosed by a chain-link fence, with patches of grass struggling for survival, and no trees or shrubs. The other yards were all tiny, attached to modest one- or two-storey houses covered in stucco or siding. There were no tall buildings as far as Maria could see. Nothing like the buildings silhouetted against the skies of Vinnytsia. The street was criss-crossed with power lines. There were no people. She began to cry. She had never, even when she was in the camps, seen a place so desolate, so small, so uninviting as Timmins.

Halina came out. "Mama, are we going to live here now?"

"Yes."

Halina saw the tears. "Here, Mama." She held out a sloppy mess of orange peel and fruit.

Maria smiled and hugged her daughter. Was this her destiny now? This bleak town in the middle of nowhere? Was Frank here? It had been three years since she had last seen him. Did he remember her? Did he still love her?

She heard Stan in the kitchen. She felt nothing for him. She couldn't believe fate had dealt her another miserable hand. The war was bad enough, but at least that had ended. Life with Stan could stretch out for years, decades. She was only twenty-six. Was she fated to live in this wilderness for the rest of her life? Maria swatted away a mosquito.

Stan worked in the forests around Timmins for the Abitibi Pulp and Paper Company. He was a logger, cutting down trees in the winter and doing odd jobs in the summer. During the winter months, the busiest time for loggers, he was in a camp deep in the woods during the week and only home at weekends. At least the pay was good and put food on the table.

For Maria, Timmins was what she imagined the Wild West to be from the movies—a small, tough town, not of cowboys but of loggers and miners. The men worked hard, drank harder, and fought at the slightest wrong. They hunted and fished for extra food and for the sheer joy of showing off their skills. They sweated in the summer, battling black flies and mosquitoes. They froze in the winter, battling frostbite and colds.

A week after Maria and Halina had arrived, Stan came home from work and announced, "Maria, look who I found on the street! Some Polak looking for pierogi." Stan laughed and pushed Frank into the apartment.

Maria almost dropped the pan she was holding. Halina hid behind her skirt.

"Hello, Maria. Welcome to Timmins." Frank gave her a chaste kiss on the cheek.

"I didn't think I'd see you here," was all Maria could say, her eyes wide with astonishment.

"Why not? I said I was going to Timmins. How was the journey?"

Stan was busy pouring vodka as Maria and Frank made small talk, never taking their eyes off each other.

"Frank's staying for supper," Stan said. "He's been very helpful since I got here. Showed me everything I needed to know. He's a big-shot gold miner now."

As Stan slopped vodka into three glasses, Maria wondered why he had never mentioned Frank before. Stan kept an eye on Frank and Maria. Were they looking at each other a bit too long? *Nah*, he thought. *It's just that Frank hasn't seen her for years.*

"Let's toast to our new life," said Stan. "To Timmins. To mining. To logging. To making lots of money."

FRANK STARTED COMING AROUND during the week when Stan was away. Soon they were lovers. Frank began pressuring Maria to leave Stan. Maria couldn't make up her mind whether to go or not. She loved Frank, but she was afraid he would turn out just like Stan.

Maria decided that was a chance she was willing to take. She was bored and frustrated. Sure, Stan worked hard, but there was never enough money for anything except food, rent, and, of course, vodka. When he went to work in the bush, he never left her much money. She was stuck in their apartment with Halina. Her daughter followed her like a little love-struck puppy.

Maria hated Timmins. The town was dominated by French Canadians and the British. She could feel them looking down on her. She didn't speak English, so there could be no socializing with them. But there were parties and dances at the Ukrainian Hall and the Polish White Eagle Club. They often turned out the same—too much alcohol, which led to somebody saying something, which led to the other person being offended, which led to the inevitable fight.

Still, Maria didn't mind the dances and parties in the halls with the other DPs. It was something to do and gave her a chance to show off, to flirt, but there was always a price to pay if Stan caught her. Occasional slaps had progressed to beatings. Maria was always anxious when Stan returned from the bush camps, where alcohol was banned. He would throw his bag in the corner of the kitchen, refuse food, and sit sullenly at the table, drinking. She lived in fear of his temper.

She understood that he'd been scarred by his experiences in the prison camps—abused, struggling to survive, seeing friends die. *Okay, Stan, I know you have your demons*, she would think, *but you know what? So do I.* She'd tried to leave her bad memories in Germany. The war was over. She was in a new country. And she wanted a new life, free of the shadows of the past. She wanted to live and have fun. She longed for ballet, opera, fine restaurants, and a man who would appreciate her. She didn't want to have to drag her drunken husband home, past vomiting fellow countrymen, every time they went to a community event.

Finally, in early April 1952, Maria had had enough— enough of Stan's drinking, enough of Stan, period, and certainly enough of Timmins. She told Frank she was ready to leave. *He's the one*, she told herself. He would protect her and Halina and be the knight in shining armour she yearned for. She and Frank just had to pick the right moment to make their getaway.

That moment came two weeks later, when Stan went on a weekend bender with some fellow Poles. He showed up for work Monday morning hungover, so he wasn't paying attention when a crane swung a log off the back of a truck. The log slammed into his back. Stan fell face down into the dirt and woke up in the hospital.

He was lucky his back wasn't broken, but he'd fractured a couple of bones. He had to stay in hospital for a couple of weeks to assess the damage and have time to heal, but the doctors were pretty sure he'd make a good recovery.

Maria and Halina visited Stan every day for a week while Frank headed south to Sudbury, where he found a job as a miner at Falconbridge Nickel Mines. He told no one in Timmins, just quietly quit his job and told his landlord he'd be leaving.

Early in May, while Stan was still in the hospital, Frank slipped into Maria's apartment as she was packing in the kitchen. He slid his arms around her waist as she was taking cutlery out of a drawer.

"I love you, Maria. Everything will be all right."

Halina stood on her tiptoes and peered into the drawer. "Mama, will you leave some for Tata?"

"Yes."

Maria told Halina they were going away with Frank.

"Far away?"

"Yes. To a new city. Sudbury. You'll love it."

"Is Tata coming?"

"No, he isn't."

"Why?"

"Because Frank will be your new Tata now."

"Oh."

After Maria packed her two suitcases, the three of them took a taxi to the train station. Halina looked back at the house on Birch Street as the taxi pulled away. Maria stared straight ahead, clutching Frank's hand.

The train to Sudbury left an hour later. Maria sat beside Frank, resting her head on his shoulder. For the first time in nine years, she let herself hope—that she and Halina could build a happy home with Frank, that she could start having some fun again, and most importantly, that this time she had chosen the right man.

MARIA WAS HAPPY in Sudbury. She and Frank were crazy in love. They couldn't keep their hands off each other. No more DP camps, no more constant surveillance by officials, no more being scrutinized by other DPs, no more long, lonely days and nights in Timmins, and no more beatings from a man she didn't love. Frank had rescued her.

Maria was mesmerized by the shops, the movie theatres, and the restaurants in Sudbury. True, there weren't many by big-city standards, but there were more than in Timmins. Europe was old, whereas everything in Canada was newer, bigger, brighter. She wanted it all.

She worked hard as a cook in a boarding house, just as Frank worked hard in the mine. At first it was all right that Frank took all the money and never spent any, never let her buy the pretty things she wanted in return for her hard work. They had their love.

Even the tar-papered shack they rented in the backyard

of a large rooming house could not ruin her happiness. It had no running water and no toilet, so Maria, Frank, and Halina had to use the toilet in the basement of the rooming house during the day. At night, they used a jumbo Crisco lard bucket with a piece of plywood covering it. Nevertheless, the shack was a perfect love nest.

But over time Maria grew tired of dragging buckets of water whenever she wanted to wash or have a cup of tea. She grew tired of peeing in the Crisco bucket at night. This was most definitely not what she wanted.

Life improved for a while when Frank came home with a second-hand Cadillac. It announced that they were doing just fine. But they weren't.

"Frank, I'm so tired of carrying these buckets of water. Can't we move to an apartment where we have running water? And a real toilet?"

"Maria, it's too expensive. We have to save our money."

"Well, how much money did you save buying the Cadillac?"

"You need a car in Canada."

"Sure, but a Cadillac? Why didn't you get a Chevy or a Ford? Why do you always get what you want, and I never get what I want?"

"Ach, stop it, Maria. When we get more money, you'll get what you want."

After that, Maria started treating herself, buying little things like a blouse, a slip, some makeup, with money she kept from Frank. She hid her treasures from him and swore Halina to secrecy.

Frank saved their money and bought a small café that served Canadian food—chips, hamburgers, hot dogs, and pies. Maria was the cook, server, and cleaner, but neither she nor Frank had any business experience, and it wasn't long before the café went bust and Maria went back to the boarding house.

That failure didn't stop Frank from looking for other money-making schemes.

"Maria, you're so beautiful," he said, holding up a new, expensive camera. "Look, we can make some easy money, and we don't even have to leave home. I'll take some pictures of you and send them to this magazine. Here, look. It's called *Playboy*."

Maria flipped through the magazine. "You want me to pose nude?"

"No, you don't have to pose nude. Just in your underwear."

Maria considered the proposition. She didn't like the idea of posing, but the money would be nice. Perhaps then they could afford a better place to live. So she stripped down to her panties and bra, and put on high heels and makeup. She lay down on their old couch, which she had bought at a second-hand store and covered in chintz fabric. She put one hand behind her head, bent one leg, wet her lips, and looked provocatively at the camera.

She didn't make Playmate of any month.

Maria's passion for Frank began to ebb. He was obsessed with getting rich, but he was a penny-pincher, a country boy who just wanted to go fishing and hunting.

He had no interest in theatre, movies, opera, dancing. He didn't have much of an education, but he was creative. He'd rather make something than spend money buying it.

Apart from their lovemaking, Maria and Frank were discovering they had little in common. And their lovemaking was not as exciting as it had been when they'd had to hide it from Stan.

Maria was bored. Her life in Sudbury was starting to suffocate her.

Chapter 15

Alone at the Station

It was all Father Jatalksi's fault. *He was the one who ruined my life*, thought Maria. His air of privilege, his easy Catholic life, annoyed her most days, but today she was truly fed up with him. She wasn't brought up with any religion, and Father Jatalksi's constant lecturing about going to church or to hell irritated her to no end. Yes, what happened was definitely Father Jatalksi's fault.

It was Sunday. Frank was working a shift at Falconbridge Nickel Mine, while Maria had the day off from cooking at the boarding house a couple of blocks away from the three-room, tar-papered shack in the backyard of the rooming house. The landlord had laid down narrow wooden planks to form a path from the basement of the rooming house to the shack for them to transport their pails of water every day. That Sunday it had rained heavily all morning, resulting in a stinking-hot, muggy afternoon. The backyard was a giant mud hole. As Maria navigated the wooden planks, balancing a pail of water in each hand, sodden earth squished over the boards with every step. The water from the pails sloshed around her legs as she struggled to keep her footing.

She was sweating. Her hair was in her eyes. She was so focused on placing one foot in front of the other without spilling a drop that she didn't see Father Jatalksi until they were almost nose to nose. He had been visiting Maria's neighbour in the shack next door. The narrow plank groaned, sinking deeper into the mud under their combined weight.

Father Jatalksi held out his right hand with his gold signet ring for her to kiss. "Good afternoon, Pani Użarowska." The priest smiled. Maria and Frank had agreed she would use his name and pretend they were married.

Maria glared at his hand, then his face, and hissed, "Get out of my way." She stepped toward the startled priest and kept walking.

Father Jatalksi had no choice but to leap off the plank into a puddle of water. His mouth was open, his hand still extended, as Maria slogged her way home. By the time she reached her tiny, waterless kitchen, her pails were only half full. Maria put them down next to a small wooden table with a white enamelled wash basin. She flung herself on the couch and burst into tears. This was not what she had imagined when she ran away with Frank. A tar-paper shack, with no running water, no toilet, endless shifts at the boarding house, and the man she loved turning into a penny-pinching scrooge. And Halina. Where was her daughter anyway? Probably running wild in the woods behind the shack as usual.

Maria felt caged. She was almost thirty. Where had her life gone? She got up and poured water into the basin. She splashed her face and examined herself in the mirror. Yes, she was still beautiful. She still got admiring looks from the men in the boarding house, but for how much longer?

She usually ignored the men, but Walter had caught her eye. He was tall, blond, a soldier from Warsaw. He was always talking about leaving the mines for a better life in Toronto.

"Plenty of opportunity in Toronto," he often told Maria. "The city needs all kinds of workers. And it's so much fun, Maria. Lots of theatres, movies, dancing, stores, and restaurants. Oh, Maria, the restaurants! With food from all over the world. You could eat in a different country every night."

Then one day Walter had lowered his voice and stepped closer to her. "You know I like you. A lot. Come on, Maria. Let's go to Toronto. You and me together. We'll have so much fun."

"Ach, Walter, you're talking nonsense. I have a child. What would I do with her?"

"Leave her with Frank." Walter smiled. "Get your bearings in the city, and then we can come back for her later."

Maria had turned back to packing lunches, but she sneaked a look at Walter as he left the boarding house, whistling.

Maybe Walter was right. She had hitched her wagon to two farm boys—first Stan and now Frank. What did they know of the finer things in life, the things Maria wanted? Theatres, dancing, restaurants, and clothes in the latest fashion. More than anything, Maria wanted fun. The Nazis had stolen her youth from her, but there was still time. She was still good-looking. And she was attracted to Walter. He understood her needs. He would take care of her.

Maria dried her face and looked at herself in the mirror with new determination. There was no future for her in Sudbury with Frank. She was going to have fun. She'd come back for Halina later. She trusted Frank to take care of her.

Maria and Walter made their plans to leave while Frank was working and Halina was playing in the woods. Maria packed her prettiest dresses, her sexiest underwear, and the money she had kept from Frank, and left.

Toronto was everything she imagined. Walter got them a small room near Queen Street and Kensington Market. It was an immigrant section of town, teeming with DPs. Walter knew some other Poles, and life soon became a big party. Maria loved it all. While Walter was looking for work, she would explore the city and go to the market to buy goodies—creamy pastries, warm, chewy bagels, fresh fruit, sliced German Black Forest ham, and Polish kielbasa. At night, she and Walter would drink, dance with other Poles, and make love. Maria's head was spinning with the delights of the big city. She had forgotten Frank and Halina.

One day, as she was leaving a delicatessen on Queen Street, she stopped abruptly, almost dropping her package on the sidewalk. There, across the street, was Stan. She hadn't seen him for three years. Maria and Stan froze on opposite sides of the street, staring at each other.

Maria almost didn't recognize Stan. He was muscular, but there were heavy bags under his eyes. Stan almost didn't recognize Maria, either. She was wearing a fancy dress, high heels, and lipstick, and her hair was styled in the latest fashion. She looked like a model.

Maria made the first move. She stepped off the curb toward him, but Stan turned away, walked briskly to a waiting car, and drove off. Maria just stood in the street, her mouth gaping. A car horn forced her back onto the sidewalk. Maria stood there for a long time. She felt her face flush with shame as she remembered how she had left him. And now Stan wouldn't speak to her. Stan had run away from her. Suddenly Maria felt guilty. She wanted Halina.

That night, she told Walter they had to go back to Sudbury and get Halina. She didn't tell him about running into Stan.

"Why do you want to get Halina? I'm sure she's fine with Frank. Aren't you having fun with me?" Walter enveloped her in a hug, nuzzling her neck.

"Stop it, Walter. She's my daughter, and if we're to be a family, I need her here."

"But, Maria, there's not enough room."

"We'll make room, or we'll get a bigger place."

"Okay, okay," said Walter, throwing his hands up.

They took the train to Sudbury on a morning when Frank was at work and Halina at school. There would be just enough time to take Halina out of school, throw her clothes in a suitcase, and catch another train back to Toronto. Walter stayed behind at the train station as Maria walked briskly up the hill.

"Mama, Mama!" Halina squealed as her mother and the school principal came into her classroom. While the principal spoke quietly to the teacher, Maria hugged Halina and led her out of the school. They were practically running.

"Mama, Mama, where are we going?"

"Home to pack your things, and then on a new adventure. You like adventures, don't you, Halina?"

"Yes," said Halina, hesitantly.

"Well, this adventure is in Toronto. A big, big city. We're going to have so much fun. We're going to live with Walter."

"Who's Walter?"

"He's going to be your new Tata."

"But I like my old Tata."

"Don't worry, you're going to love Walter. Hurry now, we have to meet Walter at the train station. Isn't that going to be fun—going on a train to Toronto?"

But when Maria and Halina returned to the train station, Walter was gone, and so were the return tickets to Toronto. Maria searched everywhere for him, but deep down she knew her adventure had come to an end. Walter must have figured he was too young to be saddled with a child. There were plenty of other women as beautiful as Maria. She returned to the bench where Halina was sitting with her bag, sat down beside her daughter, and stared vacantly at the train tracks.

"Mama, what's wrong?"

"Everything is wrong."

"Where's Walter?"

"I don't know."

"Are we going to catch a train?"

"I don't think so. Not today. Maybe never."

Maria sighed heavily. Here it was again: the crappy hand fate was always dealing her. Why couldn't something good happen to her? Just once.

"Mama, Mama." Halina shook her mother's arm. "Mama, I'm hungry. Can we go home?"

Maria looked down at Halina. She got up, picked up her suitcase, took Halina by the hand, and started walking back to Frank.

When Maria got back to the shack, she sat on the couch and waited for Frank to come home. Halina went to play in her secret places in the woods. She didn't understand what was happening, why her mother was suddenly back, why she had been taken out of school, but she could feel that something bad was about to happen, and she didn't want to be there when it did.

Maria couldn't believe Walter had left her. Why had she even gone with him? Oh yeah, it was because of that priest, Father Jatalksi. That's right. If he hadn't pressured her to kiss his ring that day, if he hadn't made her think of all the things she was missing, she would never have left Frank. It was the priest's fault for making her feel unworthy, small. It was his fault she'd turned to Walter for consolation. All she wanted was to have fun.

Chapter 16

War and Peace

Maria knew it was going to be bad after she went back to Frank. And it was. He was furious and unforgiving. She had betrayed him, but, more importantly, she had made him look like a fool. Yet he couldn't bring himself to throw her out. Instead, he ignored her and began a tit-for-tat affair with their landlady's daughter that he flaunted in Maria's face. Now it was Maria's turn to be furious, but she couldn't do anything about it.

Frank's affair ended in a couple of weeks after the landlady's daughter figured out he was using her for revenge. So Maria and Frank, rejected by their lovers, with mutual affairs under their belts, began battling in earnest, like two prizefighters, circling each other, watching and waiting for a chance to land a punch or jibe. They sparred, lashing out with verbal abuse and threats. Their chosen weapons were words and tears. Only once did Frank step outside their unspoken rules.

"Mama!" wailed Halina, standing in her pyjamas at her bedroom door. She'd been woken by shouting and witnessed Frank slap Maria.

"Go back to bed! Shut the door!" shouted Maria and Frank, almost in unison.

Each bout ended with them retreating to their corners, nursing a sullen silence until the next round. It was a couple of months before they cautiously resumed their lives, but life was never the same. Maria and Frank were never the same.

When Maria met Walter, she had thought she had found a way out. Walter was the polar opposite of Frank. He was fun, and for a brief time Maria lived the life she wanted and felt she deserved. But in the end Walter abandoned her, leaving her no choice but to pick up the pieces of her life with Frank.

The truth was, Maria was terrified of being alone. All her life, she'd had someone telling her what to do. First Aniela and Sergei. Then the Nazis. Then Stan, Frank, and Walter. Yes, Maria was terrified. She had a child. How could she care for Halina, get a well-paying job, and create a nice home without someone helping her?

Maria was forced to return to Frank and face his wrath. Better that than be alone in a new country she had lied to get into. What would happen if someone found out? Who could she turn to if she was alone?

After the fighting over the affairs ended, Maria and Frank declared a shaky truce. Every now and then, they would snipe at each other to make sure the other one knew how hurtful they had been. Frank put a stop to Maria's shopping sprees. He controlled the money. He controlled the car. He controlled her life.

Finally, a year and a half later, Maria couldn't take it anymore. She had done a lot of thinking. Maria realized she had survived a war, slave labour, bombings, a move to another country, and an abusive husband. She had fooled Americans and Canadians with her new identity. She was strong. She could fend for herself and Halina. She didn't need Frank anymore. She was done. She announced they needed a time out and she was moving to Toronto, this time with Halina.

Frank tried to discourage her, but Maria was adamant. At the end of the summer of 1958, a subdued Frank drove Maria and Halina to Toronto in the Cadillac.

Maria found work as a housekeeper for a wealthy Jewish family. She and Halina settled into a three-room apartment on the top floor of a house in the immigrant section of Toronto. They had to share a bathroom with two other women on the floor, but Maria consoled herself with the thought that at least she had a toilet now, and a kitchen with running water.

Halina started at a new school and found new friends. Maria was dating, but nobody interested her. When she came home at night after a date, Halina would be peering through the window, waiting for her mama. It made Maria happy.

As Maria was reclaiming her life, Frank found he couldn't live without her. He began visiting every weekend.

Eventually, they resurrected their relationship. The passion was gone, but they knew they needed each other to survive in Canada. They were better together. They could still have a good life.

In July 1959, Frank picked up Maria and Halina in Toronto and drove them back to Sudbury.

Chapter 17

Fathers and Daughters

Maria was pleased with the new apartment Frank had rented. It was on the second floor of a home in a respectable area of Sudbury that was dominated by first-generation Canadians, not DPs. There were two bedrooms, a living room, a bathroom with a real toilet, tub, and sink, a kitchen with a stove and fridge, and a little sitting area at the top of the stairs. The apartment even had a private entrance, but most important of all for Maria, it had hot and cold running water.

In this new neighbourhood, nobody knew she and Frank weren't married. Nobody questioned her, and she didn't confide in anyone. Her secrets were safe. Her lies were safe. The longer Maria was in Canada, the more convinced she was that her deceptions would not be discovered. She felt confident enough to go to Toronto on her own with Halina, especially since they had become Canadian citizens before they left Sudbury. On Valentine's

Day 1958, Maria and Halina officially became Canadians. Frank had become a Canadian citizen two years earlier.

But there was still a loose end in Maria's tangled web of deceptions: her parents. The last time she had written to Aniela and Sergei was from Camp Tikvah. That was eleven years ago.

During her early days in Canada, Maria had worried that the Soviet secret police would find her and drag her back to Ukraine. She had heard of a Russian couple who immigrated to the Netherlands after the war. They lived in Holland for four years before the Soviet secret police found them and forcibly repatriated them to the USSR. They were declared traitors and sent to work in the gulags of Siberia. Maria shivered when she thought about the fate of the people in those labour camps. She vowed she would never go back. She would die before setting foot in another camp.

Maria knew that her letters home from Würzburg during the war, and from the camps after the war, were monitored by the Soviets. Once she got to Canada, she stopped writing altogether. Her life was too busy, and—she rationalized—writing to her parents could make life difficult for them. The Soviets were suspicious of any letters from the West.

But, most importantly, she didn't write because she was ashamed. If her parents knew what she had done, they would be shocked. She had lied about her nationality and renounced her family name. She had stolen her mother's identity, possibly putting Aniela at risk. She had run away from her husband. She was living "in sin" with Frank. She'd had an affair with Walter. She worked as a maid and as a cook in a boarding house in Canada. It was a far cry from the pharmacist her parents had hoped she would become.

And she was struggling to be a mother herself. Halina was growing up to be an impossible teen. Parenting had been easier when Halina was younger, when Maria was in control. She vowed she would never spoil Halina the way she had been spoiled by Aniela and Sergei. The golden daughter who had grown up with everything became a mother whose favourite word was "no."

When Halina was eight: "Mama can I have a bike?"

"No! You'll fall and break your neck. It's too dangerous."

When Halina was seven: "Mama, I want to be a ballerina. Can I take ballet lessons."

"No! You're too old. You have to start ballet when you're three."

When Halina was six: "Mama, can I go to church? They're building a Polish church across the street."

"No. There is no God."

Halina never got a bike, she never got ballet lessons, but when it came to going to church, Halina threw a hysterical tantrum. Maria gave in to her headstrong daughter, and Halina started going to the Polish Catholic church across the street. For six years, Halina went to Mass faithfully, sang songs in Polish and Latin in the choir, and went to catechism classes.

When Halina had her First Communion, Maria and Frank reluctantly went to the church to witness the event.

Afterward, the family posed for professional pictures, Maria and Frank unsmiling, stiffly flanking Halina in her bride-of-Christ Communion dress, her hands clasped in prayer in front of her, looking smugly at the camera.

After Halina's First Communion, Maria was depressed. This was not the life she had envisioned for herself. She thought about writing to her parents but couldn't do it. What did she have to write home about? Her deceptions? Her failed marriage? Her turbulent life? Her struggles with motherhood? All of this, she convinced herself, would put an end to her role as the golden daughter. Better not to write. Better to just keep going. Maybe things would get better.

And there was another reason she didn't want to write to her parents. Deep down, in a dark corner of her heart, Maria blamed Aniela for sending her to school on that accursed day. She blamed Sergei for not rescuing her from the Nazis at the brick factory. Her rational mind told her she shouldn't blame them. They had no choice. The abduction would have happened anyway. The Nazis were grabbing everyone they could to work in Germany as they began losing the war. The war was not Aniela's and Sergei's fault. But still, Maria felt betrayed. Her parents should have done more to save her. The golden daughter was angry for a long, long time.

So Maria kept her secrets, her lies, her life to herself. Aniela and Sergei were old now. The truth would break their hearts. Maria convinced herself doing nothing was in everyone's best interest.

Meanwhile, in Vinnytsia, Aniela and Sergei were desperate for news—any news—of Maria. Where had she been all these years? They were used to waiting years for Maria's letters. When Maria was in Würzburg, she wrote or they got snippets of news from Valya's mother, but after Würzburg, there were no letters for five years. Then, after the war, Maria wrote from the camps. But when she went to Canada, she stopped writing—again.

Aniela was convinced Maria was dead. Not Sergei, though. He began searching. In 1960, he appealed to the Red Cross to help him find Maria. Months later he got a reply. The Red Cross gave Sergei an address on Birch Street in Timmins, Ontario, Canada. Sergei wrote immediately. Then he and Aniela waited. Weeks passed, and then a letter came. But it was his letter, the one he had sent, the one that carried his dream of reconnecting to his Musin'ka. Scrawled across the envelope: *Not at this address. Return to sender.*

Aniela cried, but Sergei became more determined. He wasn't giving up. He wrote more letters to the Red Cross and three years later got another address: Mrs. Maria Żebrowska in Sudbury, Ontario, Canada. He had found his golden daughter.

On August 18, 1963, Sergei wrote: *Our Dear Musin'ka! Today Mama and I are having a great holiday in our souls!*

Aniela wrote: *Not for a single minute have we forgotten about you, but I just thought that you were not among the living anymore, but your dear dad disproved my thoughts. He would say: "Musya lives, and I will find her."*

Maria stared at the letter. It was addressed to her using her married name, Stan's name. In Canada, she was Maria Użarowska. Sergei and Aniela had found her. Part of her was relieved. She missed her parents. She knew she would have to write back. She knew she would have to lie.

Once they started writing to each other again, Sergei became a nuisance to Maria. He was too nosy. Like Aniela, he was thrilled to be in communication with his daughter again, but he wanted to know more, especially about Stan. On August 18, 1963, Sergei wrote:

Tell us, in detail, about your dear husband: How is his health? Where does he work? Is he in correspondence with his family? Had I known the address of your husband's family, we would not have had to spend so much time looking for you all, because your husband, most likely, did not lose touch with his family, and we assume that he writes to them very often, and that they knew the exact address.

Maria contemplated the implicit reprimand in these questions. *Who is he to be telling me off?* she fumed. To Sergei, Maria would always be the young daughter he last saw behind the barbed-wire fence at the brick factory. He couldn't help her then, so now he was trying to reclaim his role as father. The more Maria studied the letter, the more annoyed she became. Her father had no right to scold her. She was now a thirty-eight-year-old mother. And, yes, she was still angry and hurt that he had left her at the brick factory. But Sergei couldn't see that:

Being a mother yourself now, you will be able to relate to how we are feeling, he wrote. *Undoubtedly, you will also be very glad, when you receive this letter from us and find out that Mama and I are, thank God, alive and well!*

Aniela and Sergei were overjoyed to find Maria again. They sent gifts: a samovar, linens embroidered by Aniela, a golden velvet table covering, and some cutlery. Their appetite for news from Canada was insatiable, especially news of their granddaughter, whom Sergei called "his golden Halinochka."

Ha, thought Maria. *If only they knew what a piece of work she's becoming.*

Teenage Halina was focused on clothes, hair, and boys. She was always challenging Maria and Frank. She was troublesome, and nosy. One Sunday afternoon, Halina was bored and began poking around Maria's bedroom. She said she was looking for a scarf. She opened a drawer and, under a pile of nighties, found a brown leather zippered office bag. She looked around. Maria was in the kitchen; Frank was in the living room.

Quietly, Halina removed the bag and sat on the bed. She unzipped it slowly. Inside was a stash of faded papers, some of them thin onion skin. As Halina read, she realized these were Maria's camp documents.

There was a document for good behaviour, a document for goods loaned to Maria in the camps, and documents saying she and Halina could immigrate to Canada. Halina even found a picture of herself stapled to her immigration document. She was four years old, her shoulders hunched almost to her ears, staring at the camera, frightened about what was going to happen.

One of the documents was on fragile onion skin and folded three times. Halina carefully unfolded it. It was a carbon copy of an original document from La Guardia camp in Germany. Halina's eyes widened. It was her birth certificate.

As she read, she became confused. In the space for father, it said Stanisław Żebrowski. *Stanisław Żebrowski!* thought Halina. *Wait a minute. Tata's name is Frank Użarowski. He's my father, so who was this Stanisław Żebrowski?*

Halina sat on Maria's bed. The penny was dropping. All her life, she had never questioned why she was Halina Żebrowska, but Tata was Frank Użarowski and Mama was Maria Użarowska. She had always dismissed the discrepancy as one of those Polish things with names.

Clutching her birth certificate, she marched into the living room. Frank was lying on the couch, reading the newspaper.

"Tata?"

"Yeah."

"Who's Stanisław Żebrowski?" Halina held her breath and shoved the birth certificate in front of his paper.

Frank didn't move. He didn't even lower the newspaper. "Go ask Mama."

Halina stomped to the kitchen. Maria was chopping carrots for supper.

"Mama," Halina said, holding up the certificate, "who's Stanisław Żebrowski?"

Maria stood still. She didn't look at the paper Halina was waving in her face. "Go ask Tata."

"Mama! Tata said to ask you. Who is Stanisław Żebrowski?" Halina demanded.

Maria kept chopping carrots.

Halina started reading the certificate out loud. "And why do they say here you were Maria Kotecka? I thought you said your maiden name was Brik."

"Stop asking so many questions."

"But Mama ..."

"No more questions." Maria was still chopping the carrots, but her hands were shaking.

"Honestly! Nobody tells me anything in this house. Well, I don't care!"

Halina stomped out of the kitchen. Maria didn't move from the chopping board. Frank stayed on the couch.

Halina put the certificate back in the leather bag, zipped it up, threw the nighties over it, and banged the drawer shut. She stormed into her room, slamming the door. Why would they never tell her anything?

Halina had no idea how deep the vein of deception ran through her family.

Chapter 18

Killarney

Maria and Frank never talked to Halina about her birth certificate, and Halina never brought it up again. The three of them retreated into an uneasy truce. Halina tucked the mystery of Stanisław Żebrowski away in her head. But she was determined to someday find out the truth.

Halina was in high school and eager to keep up with the in-crowd. To do that, she needed the latest fashions, shoes, and makeup.

"Mama, I just saw the cutest shoes at Anita's downtown. They were red with a Mary Jane strap and bow and low heels. They're only $4.77. Can I get them, please, Mama?"

"No. They're too expensive. We don't have enough money."

"We never have enough money," pouted Halina.

"Well, get a job. Make your own money."

"I'm too young. I'm only fifteen."

"You're going to be sixteen soon. Want me to talk to Lila? She's working in the kitchen at Kresge's, and she says they always need help."

"I don't want to work in a stupid kitchen at Kresge's. That's not cool."

"Okay, so no shoes."

Halina thought about it for a minute. "All right, talk to Lila."

Halina got a job as a kitchen helper at Kresge's department store. Soon her boss put her in charge of the soda fountain, making ice cream floats and sundaes. Then Halina became a short-order cook, flipping burgers and hot dogs. Finally, she got the star job. She was a waitress in charge of a whole horseshoe-shaped lunch counter, making tips on top of her salary. But she cringed at the pale-green nylon uniform, apron, and peaked hat. The cool girls at her high school wouldn't be caught dead dressed like that, or working at Kresge's.

But Halina was a good worker and found she liked the job. It got her out of the house, and she made her own money. Mama and Tata let her keep her earnings. After she got her first paycheque, Halina bought the shoes at Anita's. The girls at school were impressed.

When Maria and Frank had run away to Sudbury in 1952, the city was swarming with DPs—worker ants labouring underground for its greatest treasure: nickel. Sudbury sat on top of the biggest vein of nickel in the world, enough to keep two mining companies, Inco and Falconbridge, in business for decades.

The DPs worked hard, they played hard, and many had big dreams of making it rich. Why not? The fifties and sixties were pregnant with second chances, new beginnings, and renewed hope for better lives, certainly better than the ones left behind in the ruins of Europe. If you were willing to work hard, they told themselves, you too could have it all. Many tried. Some succeeded.

Maria and Frank came up with idea after idea for getting rich. They all failed. The café they bought went bust. The photos of Maria in her underwear for *Playboy*, a laugh. But that didn't stop them.

Maria had another scheme—mascara. She had always made her own during the war years. She'd blend soot and candle wax together to form a gooey, black mess and pour it into a little container. Once it hardened, she would spit on a brush, run it over the mascara, and apply it. But not before she forced her eyelashes upwards expertly with a small dull paring knife. Halina loved watching Maria's beauty routine.

For a while, Maria lived with her friends John and Margaret in Southern Ontario while she worked in a factory, trying to make ends meet. She showed their daughter Zana how to make mascara and pierogi. Zana was fascinated. Maria was the perfect role model—glamorous yet practical.

Maria asked Halina, now a teenager, to write a letter to Helena Rubinstein, the Polish-American who had founded a cosmetics empire. She was positive Helena Rubinstein would buy her mascara formula because they were both Polish. Helena Rubinstein never replied.

Despite their track record of failures, Maria and Frank continued scheming how to get rich—even in their retirement. When they were snowbirds, travelling to Florida, Frank met a young couple travelling in a van similar to his, only theirs was a mobile billboard, covered in Pepsi ads. Pepsi paid the couple to drive around from event to event promoting their product.

Frank was sixty-three by then, but that didn't stop him from writing a letter to Coca-Cola, Pepsi's arch rival:

I would like to offer my services to Coca-Cola Company to undertake such a project on similar terms. I believe that my personal background and characteristics would allow me to carry out such promotional travel to the full satisfaction of Coca-Cola Company. Having unlimited time at our disposal, and no obligations, my wife and I can undertake trips to various parts of Ontario, northeastern New York, and elsewhere. I would be prepared to distribute free samples of your product and any literature that you would supply to me. I have found it very easy to talk to people from all walks of life and of various age categories.

Frank never heard back from Coke. They didn't know Frank was a people magnet. He could earn anyone's trust with a few words and an easy smile.

All of Maria and Frank's schemes to get rich failed, even their most ambitious one.

One Saturday in April 1962, Frank came home after work and announced, "Maria, we're going to Killarney next weekend."

"Where?"

"Killarney. It's on Georgian Bay. Lots of good fishing and hunting. They just opened a road in the bush from highway 69, so you can drive there now. It takes about an hour. Before, you had to go by boat or plane."

"Are we going fishing?"

"Kinda." Frank paused and looked uneasily at Maria. "I want to buy a fishing camp there."

"What?"

"There's a fishing camp for sale on an island across from Killarney. It's got a big main house and three little cabins. Lots of land. A dock, boathouse, dining room, and kitchen on the water, a big boat and a couple of small ones too."

"Are you crazy? We don't have the money. What are we going to do there?"

"We're gonna make money! Rich Americans go there all the time to hunt and fish. There's money—lots of money—to be made there, I'm telling you."

"Ach, Frank, you and your hunting and fishing."

"Look, there's a big fishing lodge there already. The Killarney Mountain Lodge. This big-shot American used to bring all his buddies there by plane."

"So what?"

"So he sold the lodge and this other company bought it because they know they're gonna make money. Don't you get it, Maria? Before, you had to fly in or go by boat to Killarney, but now, with a road, ach, everyone can go there. And they will, especially the Americans. They're crazy for hunting and fishing in Canada. This is a great opportunity for us!"

Maria sighed. Another get-rich-quick scheme. Another work-Maria-like-a-slave project. If she disagreed, it wouldn't matter. Frank would do exactly what he wanted.

So Maria and Frank drove the new dirt road to Killarney. They met the owner on the main dock in the village and rode to the property in a small motorboat over a channel of water the width of a four-lane highway.

As soon as the boat was tied to the dock, Maria was drawn to a set of stairs leading up a small hill from the beach. The seller was busy showing Frank the boats and boathouse, so Maria slipped away. At the top of the stairs, an apron of lawn encircled a two-storey white clapboard house with a small porch. At the end of the grass, trees stood guard around the house. And here and there on the lawn, like accent cushions thrown casually on a couch, were the low pink-and-grey streaked rocks of the Canadian Shield. The whole effect was of a fairy-tale house in the woods, a house you ran to for safety if Baba Yaga were chasing you.

Maria tried the front door. It was open. She stepped inside the living room, which was dominated by a tall, wide fireplace made entirely of Canadian Shield rocks. The mantel was one huge rock, three feet long, two feet wide, streaked with pinks and greys. Two large stuffed woodpeckers perched on logs, watching each other from either end of the mantel. Maria touched their feathers. *How strange.*

An ornate antique upright piano stood opposite the fireplace. Maria ran her fingers over the keys. The tinkling echoed in the empty house. *Hmmm, maybe I could teach myself to play.*

Maria explored the house. There was a dining room through a flat arch with two large doors off the living room. Off on one side of the dining room was a sun porch. An old-fashioned telephone hung on the wall—a wooden box with a mouthpiece in the centre and a separate black receiver. You had to turn a crank on the side of the box to connect to an operator. Later, Maria learned that the phone line had multiple users; two short rings and one long ring meant the call was for her. If she had to make a call, she had to wait until there was no one on the line. Someone was always talking on the phone. And someone was always eavesdropping. She learned to be discreet.

Across from the sunroom, a door led to the kitchen with an old-fashioned wood-fired cookstove. From the kitchen you could exit to a shed with a modern bathroom. Maria went back to the front door, where stairs led to the second floor. Upstairs were four bedrooms. One was a large room with three single beds in it. Two were small rooms with single beds. The last bedroom had a double bed. The rooms were clean, with homemade quilts covering the beds.

The house was old but well preserved and clean. The wooden floor on the main floor shone in the sunlight. Maria felt safe, like she was with an old friend.

She explored outside and found the property held a surprise. A path from the house led to a small rocky grotto in the woods. A statue of the Virgin Mary as Our Lady of Lourdes stood in an alcove, her features softened by snow, rain, and sun, her hands clasped in eternal prayer. Just outside the alcove, a statue of Saint Bernadette knelt, her right hand reaching out to the Virgin, the saint's face forever tilted upward in amazement and adoration. Inside the alcove, to the right of the Virgin, a crude stone altar nestled in the rock. A few wooden benches in front completed the picture. The wind rustled in the trees. The grotto breathed peace into Maria's heart.

Maria was enchanted. It didn't take long for her and Frank to invest all their money in the property. They named it the Killarney Island Lodge, hoping to lure business away from the popular, and exclusive, Killarney Mountain Lodge.

But the Killarney Island Lodge attracted very few guests. Maria didn't care. When there were no guests, no Frank or Halina, she played hooky. She would pack a sandwich and thermos of tea and drive out in one of the motorboats, past the island, out of the channel, into the sparkling waters of Georgian Bay. She would stop the engine, letting the boat drift, and pull out her fishing rod. She would sit, eat her sandwich, drink her tea, and fish. For the first time in her life, she was alone, bobbing gently under the blue summer sky, not caring where she was drifting. There was no one there to tell her what to do. She had no responsibilities. It didn't matter if she caught any fish. For a few hours the weight of her life would slip from her shoulders. Peace would ease the pain from her heart.

Maria, the girl who loved theatres, restaurants, and

city life, now craved the solace of nature. She was turning into a country girl. But her moments of tranquility were fleeting.

Maria always returned from her fishing trips sadder and resigned to her life. She was in her thirties. She and Frank worked hard for three years to make the lodge a success, but hard work was no substitute for a business and marketing plan. They had no experience with either, and they were running out of money. Just like their failed restaurant, the Killarney Island Lodge was going bust.

Its fate was sealed when Frank hurt his back working underground at the mine. He was hospitalized for a month and reassigned light duty above ground. Maria had to get a job that paid good money. She went to Waterloo in Southern Ontario and stayed with her friends Margaret and John. She got a job at the Kralinator Filters plant. Once again, she was a factory worker, standing in an assembly line for hours. But she was older now. The work took its toll on her back. *At least*, Maria thought, *this time I'm getting paid.*

Frank and Halina stayed in Sudbury. Halina went to high school and kept house. Maria came home in the spring to get ready to open the lodge for the summer and fall. It was a drain on their meagre resources, but they couldn't bring themselves to sell it. Frank liked the fishing and hunting. He still dreamed he could make a go of it.

Common sense told Maria they had to sell Killarney, but she kept pushing the idea aside. Killarney was useful when Maria wrote to her parents. She could brag that they had a second home, that they were successful. It was another deception, but Maria justified it by saying she didn't want to worry Aniela and Sergei about her true situation.

But, most of all, Killarney Island Lodge was a sanctuary for Maria. The house had put its arms around her in an embrace that wouldn't threaten her, or hurt her, or demand anything of her. For the first time since the Nazis had snatched her from behind her school desk, Maria had found some peace.

Peace that was all too brief. Now that Sergei and Aniela had found her, she had to deal with the question of her husband. So she decided to spin her most elaborate lie yet.

Chapter 19

A Tangled Web

Maria had left Stan in 1952, but she hadn't told her parents then, and she wasn't about to now, eleven years later. Instead, she told them she hadn't written sooner to protect them from the Soviets. Most of her letter described how good her life was with Stan and Halina.

Sergei was suspicious. Surely this Stanisław Żebrowski was writing to his family in Poland. If he could just get the Żebrowski family's address, perhaps he could start a relationship with the parents of his son-in-law. Sergei began pestering Maria for information about Stan's family. He knew his daughter. She would avoid or ignore direct questions. Deep down, Sergei suspected there was more going on in his daughter's life than she was letting on.

Sergei was right, but he didn't know that, by now, Maria was a pro at avoiding and lying. Maria had to distract Sergei, and what better way than with photos. *Yes, that's it*, she thought.

On April 2, 1964, Sergei wrote: *We are very grateful to you for having sent us the pictures of Stanisław, where he is represented together with his sisters. All three of them are very handsome and pleasant looking. And whoever sees this photo just admires them.*

Maria smiled as she read Sergei's letter. It wasn't Stan; it was Frank and his two sisters. Sergei and Aniela believed her. *Why wouldn't they?* she thought. They had no idea what Stan looked like. She sent more photos.

On May 1, 1964, Aniela wrote, *All the photos are charming, especially where Halinka is sitting on her dad's shoulders.* Again, those were Frank's shoulders Halina was sitting on. Maria even went to a professional photographer with Frank and sent her parents studio pictures of herself and her husband, "Stan." Maria never told Frank of the subterfuge.

Sergei gushed, *How good are we now! We are not two anymore. We are already five. We are no longer lonely. At any hour, we can talk to you in writing! We are a five-strong close family: me, Mama, you, Halinochka, and Stanisław. This knowledge inspires us greatly, and, at any price, we must live long.*

The letters and photos became a lifeline for Sergei and Aniela. Alone in Vinnytsia, their lives revolved around the fictional family in Canada. Each letter they wrote contained a plaintive plea for more pictures, more information, no matter how trivial. Aniela wrote, *Awaiting a reply like a swallow awaiting summer. Write, dear Musya.*

Maria, however, was not the only one practising the art

of deception. As the exchange of letters continued, Sergei began spinning his own web of lies that he thought would spare his daughter. He kept from her that he was going blind because of glaucoma. He kept from her that Aniela had developed breast cancer. And he kept from her the news of Aniela's death. Maria never forgave him.

Aniela died at home on March 7, 1965. She was eighty-two. Sergei held her in his arms and sobbed. But he couldn't bring himself to tell Maria her mother was dead. So he lied.

March 22, 1965—two weeks after Aniela died—Sergei wrote to his daughter: *Her courage is wonderful but she is getting weaker every day. This week has been a little better. She cheered up a little and began to eat a little. Let's hope that your mother will get better and she will live with us for many years.*

May 18, 1965—nine weeks after Aniela died—Sergei wrote: *She has severe anemia, exhaustion, and the cancer has spread to the armpit, neck, and liver. The only possible intervention is surgery, but even this rarely goes well.*

September 24, 1965—six months after Aniela died—Sergei finally indicated that Aniela was dead: *From early morning until late at night I shed bitter tears. Inexpressible grief befell you and me. Well, this is how the world is. People live to a certain age and then they leave us and new ones are born.* But he didn't say when she died.

October 22, 1965—seven months after Aniela died—Sergei finally told Maria the truth: *I have been hiding from you the fact that mommy died. I did not want to upset you.*

But Maria had suspected, ever since that first letter in

March, that her mother was dead, that Sergei was avoiding the truth. In a rare moment of self-reflection, she saw herself in her father. She realized, *I am my father's daughter.* She was good at this game of deception because she had been taught by her father. But Maria couldn't see how Sergei's flair for the dramatic also flowed in her veins. She accepted it as a family trait, one she saw in Halina but never in herself.

In his letters after Aniela's death, Sergei wrote with dramatic abandon: *I don't have and will not have my life ever again. I long for our mommy day and night, and the longing is gnawing at my heart like rust gnaws away iron.* And in another letter: *I visit her each day, but she is silent, for all my crying and weeping. I return home tired, defeated, with nobody to share and tell my grief to. In your letter, you say very rightly that this is how the world is made up, and that all humans are mortal. But still, that does not make it any easier for us to bear.*

Maria mourned her mother's death without any fuss. She was sad, but since she had moved to Canada, Vinnytsia and her parents seemed so far away. Had Sergei not gone to such lengths to find her, she probably never would have reached out to her parents. Her life was just too busy to write, she kept telling herself. But it was an excuse. Maria wanted to forget about Vinnytsia, her abduction, the brick factory, and all the horror and humiliation she had suffered. Most of all, she wanted to forget the anger she harboured against her parents. Deep down, Maria believed everything that had happened to her was their fault. But what good would it do now to bring up the past? Best not to talk about it.

But she was happy Aniela had a good funeral. Sergei wrote: *Our mommy is buried on a very good and honourable spot. She is surrounded by professors and actors on the first central alley of the cemetery. The funeral was very opulent. There were many people and wreaths. And in the spring, if I am still alive, I will have a good monument erected. This is all that I'm living for now.*

Two years after Sergei buried his beloved Aniela, he began writing to Maria about an old friend, a doctor, who escorted him to and from the Filatov Eye Clinic in Odessa. Maria frowned reading the letters. Sergei was at it again, she thought. He had something important to say but couldn't do it. She would have to wait. In the next letter he explained how, since he was now completely blind, his friend Taisia Semionovna was keeping house for him. Finally, in the third letter, dated January 28, 1968, Sergei dropped his bombshell.

He had married Taisia.

Maria was furious. "Unbelievable! Oh my God, what has he done?" Maria wailed, clutching Sergei's letter.

Halina came running from her bedroom, where she had been studying.

"Who? What's wrong, Mama?"

"Your grandfather. Oh my God!"

"Oh no! Did he die?"

"He should be dead for what he did."

"What?"

"He got married again!" Maria shouted. "And only three years after your grandmother died. What was he thinking?" Maria was pacing the kitchen, waving the letter around.

"Married? To whom?"

"Taisia somebody. Ach, the old fool doesn't realize she's just after his money! They all think the streets are paved with gold here. Just wait for the next letter, Halina. It's going to be a shopping list, I guarantee you."

Maria was right. Taisia took Sergei's dictation and in the next letter asked for clothes. It sounded like Sergei was asking, but Maria knew the truth. She hit the roof. She sent nothing. She shoved the letter in Halina's face.

"See! I told you she'd send a shopping list. This is her handwriting, not Papa's. He's blind, so she can write anything she wants and he'd never know it. And he can't read, so she has to read my letters to him. God only knows what she's saying. Ach, the old fool."

"I know, Mama, but think about it for a minute. He's not alone anymore. Right? Someone is caring for him. You don't have to worry about him."

"She's after his money, and ours," Maria snapped back.

"So what? You don't have to give her anything."

Maria refused to send anything to Taisia. She refused to acknowledge her. She told Sergei she and Frank needed their money for themselves.

Sergei was hurt, and their relationship became strained. A month later, he wrote back:

I realized that, although all of you work, at the same time you are very needy financially, and therefore I decided, despite my absence of eyesight, and my general condition, if you tell me that you are in need, me being your sole father, and you my sole child, I will send you assistance.

How scary and wild is it that, in response to my letter, you manage to treat my request with such rudeness. Why have you treated my friend Taisia Semionovna with such coldness? She, who is so helpful. Such a cold and rude attitude of your family toward my friend T.S. surprises me extremely.

Maria was angry with her father, but she still loved him, even though he had kept the news of her mother's illness and death from her. But she couldn't bring herself to befriend Taisia. Sergei had gone too far.

In his last letter to Maria, in 1970, he remonstrated: *I did not know that you are very busy that you can't find time to write to your only father in a timely manner. In your letter, you are not even inquiring about my health, let alone that in not one letter did you inquire about your poor mommy.*

From the moment Maria was abducted by the Nazis, Sergei had tried to maintain communication with his daughter. It had not been easy. Now, in the last stages of his life, his golden daughter, his Musin'ka, was shutting him out of her life.

She didn't tell her father that, in addition to the new home in Sudbury, they had also bought a house in Florida, which they rented out. She didn't tell her father her secret dream of moving to that house when she got older. The winters in Sudbury were getting too cold for her.

And she didn't tell her father right away that Halina, his beloved Halinochka, had gotten married. She couldn't believe it herself when Halina told her, breaking the news when they had lunch downtown during Maria's lunch break from the department store where she worked. Halina had moved out of the house when she was in her second year of university, after a fight with Maria. Halina was living in a communal house with other students. One of them was André Casaubon. Maria met him and was immediately leery of him.

At lunch, between the main course and dessert, Halina announced she was going to marry André.

Maria dropped her fork. "You're going to marry him? Halina you don't know what you're doing. How long have you known this boy?"

"Long enough to know I love him."

"What do you know about love? You're still a child. You haven't seen the things I have. If you had, you wouldn't be in such a hurry to marry the first boy that asks you."

"He didn't ask me. I asked him," Halina said smugly.

"What?"

"Yeah. We want to live together and we found a great apartment, but the landlord will only rent to married couples. The landlord also knows you and Tata, so I asked André to marry me so you wouldn't be ashamed that we were living in sin. Plus, I do love him."

"Ach, Halina, you've always been stubborn, just like your father. Just don't expect me to do anything."

"You never do anything for me anyway. You and Tata don't have to pay a penny for my wedding. We're going to City Hall on Halloween."

Maria was stunned. How could Halina do this to her? On Friday, October 31, 1969, Halina married André. Maria and Frank relented and had some of their friends, Halina's friends, and André's parents over for a reception that night.

Meanwhile, the link between Maria and her father, tenuous at the best of times, was at a breaking point, and Maria was blinder than Sergei. She couldn't see what was happening. Perhaps she didn't want to, or she just didn't care.

The next letter Maria got from Vinnytsia was from Taisia.

Her father was dead.

Your dad suffered when you told him that you have no time, that you have a family, that you can't reply to his letters. He cried a lot ... You're busy, while your dad, an old man, and sick on top of that, kept crying, kept asking you to write to him ... Dad will never again distract you from your family.

Maria put the letter down. How had it come to this? A bitter letter from a stranger, informing her of the death of her father, blaming her for letting an old, blind man die of a broken heart. What did this stupid woman know about her and her father? Maria was sad that Sergei had died, but her sorrow was overwhelmed by her anger at Taisia.

At least now she would no longer have to maintain the pretense that she was happily married to Stanisław. In her heart, Maria knew she had been deceiving her parents, but it was their fault, she told herself, because they pressured her for too much information. Now that they were gone, her lies were safe. Or so she thought.

Sergei Brik with his "golden daughter," Maria.

Maria.

Aniela Brik with her daughter, Maria.

This photograph of Maria (left) and two school friends in Vinnytsia was taken shortly before her abduction.

Photograph of Maria for her German slave ID.

Frank Użarowski in a photograph he gave to Maria in Weiden.

Stanisław Żebrowski (circled) in a German prisoner of war camp. According to Polish military records, he spent Christmas 1940 in Stalag 4B at Mühlburg.

Stanisław's father, Ignacy Żebrowski, in 1902, when he served as a bodyguard to Tsar Nicholas II at the Kremlin in Moscow.

Maria and Stanisław on their wedding day in Weiden.

Maria with Halina outside Barracks 32 in Weiden DP camp.

Frank, Maria, and Halina in Weiden DP camp, Christmas 1947. Maria had cut off a piece of the photo and always refused to tell Halina who was sitting on their right.

More than seventy-five years after this photograph was taken, Halina was given a print of the original, showing her birth father, Stanisław, on the right.

Maria with an unknown man in Bad Reichenhall DP Camp.

Halina with her doll on a stump by the Saalach River in Bad Reichenhall.

Maria, in Bad Reichenhall, channels her favourite actress, Lana Turner.

Frank, Maria, and Halina in Sudbury, shortly after Maria left Stanisław in Timmins.

Halina's grandmother Aniela Brik, as she appeared to Halina in a vision in Killarney, wearing a coat with a fur collar and a wide-brimmed hat.

Maria in her happy place, the fishing and hunting lodge in Killarney.

Halina and Frank in Sudbury, in one of the pictures
Maria sent to her parents as she maintained the
fiction that she was still married to Stanisław.

Halina at the unmarked grave of her father,
Stanisław, in Swastika Cemetery, Kirkland Lake.

Halina in the Żebrowski family home in
Nienalty, Poland, where her father was born.

The Żebrowski family reunion in Halina's
honour, Nienalty 2024.

PART III
DISCOVERY

Chapter 20

The Letters

My mother, Maria Użarowska, died on January 16, 2018. She was ninety-two. Two weeks later, I was in my office with a lifetime of documents scattered on my desk, spilling over onto the floor—official documents, camp records, and personal papers. I sat at my desk chair and looked out the window. I could see the Atlantic Ocean peeking out between the trees. My husband, Neil, and I lived on an island in St. Margaret's Bay, Nova Scotia. I had met Neil Everton, a BBC producer, in 1991, when I was covering the Gulf War as a TV news producer for the Canadian Broadcasting Corporation, the CBC, in Amman, Jordan.

At first, it was simply a professional relationship. The CBC had a contractual agreement with the BBC to share information and video. The American network NBC was part of our group. Covering major international events is an expensive proposition for a single network, so every day Neil, the NBC producer, Walter, and I met to share resources. I was used to this arrangement, as I had worked with the BBC and NBC during the Romanian Revolution. The producers changed, but not the networks.

As soon as I arrived in Jordan, I went to meet Neil at the Intercontinental Hotel, where he had set up the BBC's operation.

"Hi, I'm Halina St. James, the video whore from the CBC."

I was trying to make a joke, but Neil looked puzzled. I quickly backtracked and thrust out my hand. "Halina St. James from the Canadian Broadcasting Corporation."

"Canada, Canada," Neil mused in his posh British accent. "Don't we own you?"

And that was my first exposure to Neil's wicked sense of humour. I was not amused. We spent weeks working together in Amman and Baghdad. Eventually, we fell in love and got engaged. I kept my female buddies in the CBC's Ottawa bureau in the loop about my romance and then engagement. They were ecstatic.

"You're the CBC's first war bride," messaged Anna Maria Tremonti.

Mama had liked Neil the moment she met him. She told me, "Well, finally you got a real man." She had never really cared for André. That marriage had ended after eighteen years.

I had begun working for the CBC as a television news producer for the flagship news show *The National*, in their Montreal bureau. After two years I was transferred to

Ottawa to cover national politics and international events. I got to travel Canada and the world, reporting on history in the making. I prided myself on knowing a story when I saw one. And I was used to working under deadline pressure, sorting through notes and research documents to pick out the important from the merely interesting.

Now here I was, long retired from journalism, sitting in Halifax holding a stack of Mama's letters tied together in a bundle with string, many still in their original envelopes. The fifty-three letters were fragile, brown with age. I opened one—it was in Russian. I slipped several more out of their envelopes. Most were in Russian, a few in Polish.

My first impulse was to throw the whole lot out. I had had it with Mama. I was so tired of always having to act like her mother and live her dramas. I just wanted to clean out her stuff and get on with my life. *There's no story here*, I thought. My hand hovered over the garbage bag, but, at the last minute, something stopped me. What was in those letters? Why did she keep them all these years? Why did she never tell me about them? What secrets did the letters hide? What pain? And what stories did they tell?

I looked at the mess in my office. It was a metaphor for the last years of Mama's life. They hadn't been happy golden years. Mama and Tata were in their eighties, living on pensions, when their health began to deteriorate. They had retired and moved from Sudbury to St. Catharines, but Mama found the city too hot in the summer and the house too big. She was stuck day and night with Tata. As she aged, she relied on me more and more. Her relationship with Tata had soured to the point where they merely tolerated each other. They moved to separate bedrooms. Tata had confessed to me, "We're together because you can live better on two pensions than one." Their passion and love had dissolved into an uneasy financial deal. An unfair deal too. Tata still controlled Mama's money. He watched every move she made, every cent she spent. He forbade her to take the car out. Mama complained of feeling like a prisoner in her own home.

And then everything changed.

"I've got lung cancer," Mama announced. "I never smoked a day in my life. This is all your fault, Frank. You couldn't stand the winters in Sudbury anymore. You had to move somewhere warm. Yeah, you were the one who picked St. Catharines. It's the most polluted place in Canada!" she screamed. "Look what's around us—Hamilton, Toronto, Windsor. Nothing but factories and cars everywhere. Oh God, you and your stupid farms. You just want free fruit and honey and heat, heat, heat! We have to do everything you want! You gave me cancer!"

"Ach, shut up, Maria," Frank grumbled. "What do you know?"

"I have cancer. That's what I know, you stupid old fool! And you gave it to me!"

But Tata couldn't focus on Mama's cancer. He was descending into dementia. He slept in his van in the searing heat of summer like a cake baking in an oven. As his confusion took an ever-greater toll on him, he spent his days in his second-hand red leather recliner by the bookcase in the TV room. He built a crude shelf between the chair and the bookcase, which he piled with magazine and newspaper clippings on health cures, three or four calendars, two clocks, scraps of paper, and letters, some opened, some not. Two wristwatches were nailed to the back of the bookcase. All around him was an ever-growing mountain of scissors, screwdrivers, a small desk lamp, foot massagers, back massagers, calculators, phone books, nail clippers, and various knick-knacks.

All of this detritus was smeared with honey that dripped from an overturned, loosely lidded jar on the top shelf. Honey was Tata's fountain of youth, his miracle cure-all. He used it on everything, including his face. I found that out when I kissed him once and stuck to his cheek.

The chair became his world, and he retreated deeper and deeper into its cluttered, sticky embrace. It was buried under an old blanket, three backrests—one covered in a dirty pillowcase—a heating pad, a grimy afghan stuffed in a corner, and a frayed tea towel. Behind the chair, Tata had stashed plastic grocery bags full of vitamins, herbs, and the latest health store concoctions promising life everlasting. Many of the bottles were never opened; he forgot about them once he slipped them behind the chair.

Mama refused to touch his chair. She sat in her own chair, three feet away, staring silently at the TV—two souls bound in their mutual isolation.

When Tata's dementia was complicated by a urinary tract infection and inflammation of his esophagus, he was hospitalized. He couldn't go home because Mama was getting treatment for lung cancer and couldn't care for him. We placed him in a nursing home. In his lucid moments, he hated it. Meanwhile, Mama was alone in the house. She was eighty-six and frail. I flew out constantly to help her. She had surgery to remove the cancerous left lobe on her lung. Mama could now add cancer to her list of things she had survived, but she couldn't cope on her own, so I moved her into a seniors' residence just three blocks from Tata's nursing home. But Mama never visited Tata unless I took her.

Six months after Mama's surgery, Tata died peacefully in his bed. He was ninety years old. A friend who had stopped by to visit held his hand at the end. He told me Tata's last words were simply "Bye, bye." Among the mourners at his funeral was the mayor of St. Catharines. I had always marvelled at Tata's ability to make friends with everyone, no matter their status in life, and have long relationships with them.

I moved Mama to Nova Scotia to a one-bedroom apartment on the third floor of a luxury seniors' retirement residence with a million-dollar view, perched high on a hill in Halifax. Mama could afford the rent because, after Tata died, I found a stash of money he had hidden from her. The apartment's picture window showcased the quintessential Nova Scotia scene of sailboats, motorboats, kayaks, and canoes circling lazily on sparkling water. This was the Northwest Arm, a finger of the Atlantic Ocean pointing straight into the heart of Halifax. Across its water, Mama could see traffic flowing downtown.

She hated it. She didn't like the food—too Canadian. She didn't like the other residents—too old. She refused to join the art group—too snooty. Mama even complained about having to take an elevator to go outdoors. As for the view? It was ... okay.

I moved her to another residence when she got dementia and became aggressive. It was a small home run by a nice Polish couple. Mama had her own room and bath, but when she arrived, she took one look and sighed, "What a sad little room."

As her dementia progressed, she had to transition to a nursing home. Mama had a large room with not much of a view, just of a large tree. Its branches filled the window. She sat in her chair looking at it for hours. Once, when I was visiting, I heard Mama ask the tree, "Ach, why did Frank have to die first? Why did he go first?"

On January 15, 2018, the staff tucked Mama into bed. She gazed at the tree, her lovely tree, as they drew the curtains shut. She closed her eyes. She never opened them again.

It was a sad end to a long life. By the time she died, she had alienated every friend she had. And I was so weary of her, I didn't know whether I loved her or not. So many conflicting emotions rattled through my heart as I sat holding her bundle of letters. I was sad, but I was angry too. I was grieving, but I was relieved. I had to deal with her death—did I really want to delve back into her life? But I didn't want to throw her letters out. It was too soon.

ABOUT A YEAR LATER, I had the letters translated by a Russian friend, Marina. When she returned them, all neatly organized in a binder, she said she and her partner had cried while reading some of them. "They're mostly from your grandparents," said Marina. "They're very sad."

Still, I wasn't ready to read the letters, so I gave the binder to Neil. "Marina's right," he said. "There's such profound sadness in these letters, and so much pain too. Your grandparents were trying hard to stay connected to your mama. You have to read them."

But I still couldn't. It was too soon after Mama's death. I was done with her dramas.

My friend Anna Maria Tremonti came to visit, and I showed her the binder. She knew Mama and my struggles with her. Anna Maria flipped through it, reading sections. "Oh my god! This is gold. Honestly, what's wrong with you? This is a treasure trove. People have written books with only a fragment of the material you have. Read the letters, Halina! This is a book. Write!" With that, Anna Maria closed the binder and mimed hitting me on the head with it.

"Okay, okay," I capitulated. "I'll read the damn letters."

So I started reading snippets. The first was from my grandmother Aniela:

I so like the picture where you are with your husband, the two of you holding a fish in your arms. You are so attractive in trousers, just lovely. And that photo where Stanisław is in a boat—tell him on my behalf that I am very, very grateful to him, and that I am asking him to take more pictures more often, and to send us such photos of daily life. I love those very much.

Wait a minute—Stanisław? With Mama, holding a fish in a photo together? I checked the date of the letter: January 25, 1964. Something was wrong. By then I knew Stanisław Żebrowski was my birth father, but he'd been out of the picture since 1952, when I was four.

I grew up with Frank as my tata, not Stanisław. How could Mama send her parents a picture, twelve years after she ran off with Frank, of her with Stanisław? *Oh my God*, I realized, *Mama had simply substituted Frank for Stan.* Everything that happened to Frank, she told her parents, happened to Stan. When Frank was injured in the mine, she said it was Stan. She even gave progress reports on "Stan's" recovery in subsequent letters. I was flabbergasted at the enormity of this deception and Mama's ability to maintain it until her parents died.

So many questions came up as I dipped deeper into the letters. I cursed myself for not pressing Mama or Tata for answers when they were alive. I had been a journalist, after all. I had covered international stories for the CBC: the fall of the dictator Nicolae Ceaușescu; former prime minister Brian Mulroney's summit in the USSR; the Francophone Summit in Dakar; various Economic Summits; the Olympics in Barcelona, Lillehammer, and Atlanta. Asking questions was what I did. But I never had the inclination or the nerve to question my parents about their experiences during the war. I did try when I found my birth certificate, but neither Mama nor Tata would talk. I tried a few more times after that. No luck. So I stopped.

It wasn't until I was fifty-five years old that I had it out with Mama. We were in the backyard of her home in St. Catharine's, Ontario. It was September, still warm outside. We were sitting in lawn chairs, having a cup of tea.

"Mama, I've started searching for my father, Stanisław Żebrowski. Tell me about him."

"I don't know anything."

"You do, Mama. Stop treating me like a child and tell me about my father."

Mama was silent, so I repeated the question. My anger showed in my voice. "Where is my father?"

"I don't know, and I don't care."

"Mama, what happened between the two of you?"

Mama snapped. "You want to know the truth?" she screamed. "Okay, here's the truth. He was a violent drunk. He beat me. I had to grab you and run for our lives. I don't care where he is. But I'm telling you one thing, if you ever, ever find him, don't you dare tell him where I am!" With that, Mama went inside and slammed the door.

I didn't want to remember that day. I closed the binder of letters and sat looking at it. Clearly, there was a lot I knew nothing about. Maybe the letters had the answers I was looking for. Did I want to find out? I decided I did, but I needed a plan.

I hired a professional translator to go over the letters for nuances Marina might have missed and for context. Michael Kramer, who came from the same area of Ukraine as Mama, had worked for the federal government as a translator. He was perfect.

And so, at the age of seventy-two, a year after my mother died, I set out to learn what the letters contained. I knew I would discover some uncomfortable truths about Mama, Tata, and my grandparents. And maybe I would learn something about this Stanisław Żebrowski and his family.

Mama had secrets, so many secrets. She took them to her grave, but she left me her letters. But why had she kept them all those years? Did the woman who rarely talked about her past while she lived want me to know the truth after she died? I needed to know.

What I discovered rocked my world. I was stunned! The letters shed light on the despair and guilt my grandmother carried to her death, the sorrow and anger my grandfather felt at being abandoned by his only child, and the depth of my mother's deceptions. And they introduced me to the golden daughter. The letters told of a time when the world went mad, and how a pampered child learned to survive in the face of cruelty, hardship, and terror. And how the skills that helped her endure the war couldn't help her enjoy the peace that followed.

The more letters I read, the more astounded I became. I realized I really knew nothing about my mother's past. Nothing about her childhood in Vinnytsia, Ukraine. Nothing about her war experiences in Germany.

I cried bitter tears of guilt. *Oh, Mama, Mama. Why did you never tell me? We could have shared the burden. Maybe I could have helped you.*

I could have made her life better. I could have been a better daughter. I could have made her happy. I could have. I could have, but I didn't.

I couldn't fathom the suffering and loss my grandparents had endured after Mama was abducted by the Nazis. In one of her early letters, Aniela confessed how helpless she had been to prevent what had happened. The minute I held that letter, I felt my grandmother's pain. The letter was written with a fountain pen in Russian. I couldn't read the Russian script, but I only had to look at it to feel Aniela's anguish. Sorrow floated off the pages in clouds of unevenly written phrases, crossed-out words, crossed-out sentences. Splotches of ink littered the paper.

Aniela's letter, from August 25, 1943, was a painful confession, a plea for understanding for how she had been caught by surprise: *When you left at 8 o'clock in the morning to go to the technicum, none of us knew, neither I, nor you, that, after leaving home, you would not be back anytime soon. Oh God, what was the horror that seized us?* Aniela wrote the letter six months after the Nazis has taken her daughter. By then, she knew Mama was a slave worker in Würzburg for Dr. Schroeder and his wife. As Aniela wrote, she remembered the last time she had seen her daughter: *Exactly 6 months ago today we bade farewell to you in the camp. At that minute, I had a sparkle of hope that I would go to the railway station and up there I would be able to pluck you out, but alas, like everybody, I was powerless.*

Aniela was powerless, just like all the other parents at the train station, but it didn't stop her from convincing herself she had committed the greatest sin a mother could—failing to protect her child. Aniela was asking for forgiveness. She signed her letter, *Your bad mama*—still, she blamed herself. I stared at the letter. What a burden Aniela had chosen to carry, a burden that haunted her to her grave.

My grandfather Sergei was also haunted by the memory of those fateful days, but it took him twenty-two years to write about it. On October 22, 1965, Sergei wrote to Mama in Canada: *I always have before my eyes the vision of how you turned up behind the barbed wire with a chunk of black bread, weeping bitterly.*

For the rest of his life, Sergei kept three pictures of his daughter close by him: Mama standing alone on a chair with her golden hair cascading from the bow on top of her head. Him and his Mushin'ka in a close embrace, his face beaming with pride. And a chubby three-year-old Maria bundled up in a chinchilla fur coat with Aniela standing behind in her. These were the images Sergei wanted to remember.

Now I was haunted by this image of Mama behind the barbed wire. She was so young, snatched at gunpoint, living on scraps, and forced into slavery.

At seventeen.

At seventeen, I was in high school in Canada, goofing around with my girlfriends, focusing on boys, makeup, and the latest fashions.

I had no idea Mama was a slave worker in Germany. An Ostarbeiter. I had to look up who the Ostarbeiter were.

Of all the nationalities the Nazis enslaved in their quest for workers, it was the Ukrainian Ostarbeiter they hated the most. They considered them only one step above Jews.

Mama was just one of 5.7 million people snatched from their towns and villages and sent to work in Germany. At the beginning of the war, some of the workers were lured to Germany by the promise of having ample food and learning a trade. "Yes, yes, you will be able to go home," the Nazis told them. But as Germany began losing the war and more German men were drafted into the military, the Nazis needed more workers to keep the Wehrmacht operating. That's when the abductions started.

I wondered why there were so few stories about the slave workers in Germany. The answer was that most survivors, like Mama, didn't want to talk about their past. Many were ashamed they had been forced to work for the enemy. They wanted to forget and just get on with their lives.

Some of the slave workers who returned to the USSR were punished as traitors and had to spend years being "re-educated" in gulags, the notorious Soviet labour camps. Others were denied jobs because of their past. They were shunned in their towns and villages. Their homeland turned its back on them.

But Mama didn't experience any of that because she never returned to Vinnytsia after it was reclaimed by the Soviets. She survived the slavery, the bombs, and the chaos of peace when it came. But at what price? She never saw her parents again. She renounced her country. She struggled with two unhappy marriages. She became a mother. She made it to Canada. And she was still only twenty-six.

She must have blamed her parents for not protecting her. How could she not? She had been brought up as the pampered golden daughter. She was their miracle child, born when Aniela and Sergei were middle-aged and had lost all hope of having a child. Nothing bad would or should ever happen to her. But it did. The salutations my grandparents used were the elaborate diminutives of love-struck parents. Sergei wrote *Hello, our golden daughter Musin'ka!* or *Hello, my only ardently loved little daughter, Musin'ka* or *Hello, my dear clever daughter*. After my grandmother died, Sergei began one letter with *My dear, the only friend in the whole world, my beloved daughter Musin'ka*. My grandmother was no different, calling Mama *My dear little daughty Muysa* or *My only and dear daughty Musin'ka* or *Our dear, ardently beloved Musin'ka*.

I understood diminutives were a way of expressing intimacy and affection in Russian, but my grandparents took them to another level. They seemed archaic, even patronizing. But then I realized two things. One, all the letters were being scrutinized first by the Nazis and later by the Soviets, so Aniela and Sergei had to be careful of what they wrote. Second, I believed my grandparents found it easier to express their affection in the salutation than by saying "I love you" in the body of the letter itself. If they struggled to express their emotions, then their daughter, my mama, had inherited that trait. I have no memory of her ever holding me and saying "I love you."

As I read through the letters, the truth of my mother's life unfolded before me. For the first time, I saw the woman, not just the mother. I also got to know the grandparents I had never met. I felt their despair, their struggle to stay in contact with their only child.

I saw the lengths my mother went through to create a new identity and survive the turmoil at the end of the war. I saw the warning signs of a budding love triangle developing in the drafty wooden barracks of a displaced persons camp. I saw the lies and deceptions that shaped the life of the golden daughter.

One thing became clear: I wanted to learn more about this woman who was my mother. I knew that would help me understand myself better. And I needed to find out who my father was. What happened to him? A good place to start looking for clues was to follow in Mama's footsteps. I had to go to Germany.

Dear Grandpa Sergei,

I wish I had known you. You spoiled my mama, and I know you would have spoiled me too—your golden Halinochka. But it was not meant to be.

You adored my mama. I can't imagine your pain at seeing her for the last time, behind the barbed-wire fence at the brick factory, and at not hearing from her for years. Yet you always believed she was alive. And you eventually found her in Canada. Bravo. But by then, Grandpa, she was no longer a child. She was a woman with secrets. I don't know how she really felt about you finding her. Part of me thinks she didn't want to be found.

I wish I knew more about you. I have a picture of you as a young man. You're wearing the uniform of a well-respected school in Odessa. People from that school went on to be managers and businessmen. And yet in one of Grandma's letters she said you worked in an artel in the forest. Were you a logger, just like my father, Stanisław? That would be something.

Grandpa, I don't know much about you except you had the heart of a poet. You were a romantic. Your letters were so articulate. I think I got my passion for words and creativity from you.

And you loved me. You called me your "golden granddaughter," but Mama never told me. I only found out when I had your letters translated. You were so happy when I was born. Grandma said you bought some little socks for me, even though you knew I could never wear them. You had a soft heart for Mama, Grandma, and me.

I am so sad I never met you. I am so sad you couldn't play with me when I was little. And I am so sad I couldn't help you when Grandma was dying, and comfort you when you were left alone.

You became blind, but I believe you were always able to see us—your family, so far away. You saw us, even though we deserted you in your hour of need. I hope to make it up to you now by always holding you close in my heart.

I love you.

Your golden granddaughter,

Your Halinochka

Chapter 21

Würzburg

I stood on a cobblestone path in an abandoned rail yard in Würzburg, Germany. It was a warm day in May 2022. This path was Mama's entry point into slavery. I stood thinking about what had happened here almost eighty years ago.

Mama arrived in Würzburg in March 1943. She would have been ordered out of a cattle car after her journey from the Wolfstein Transit Camp in Neumarkt. She would have been cold. Was she frightened? Angry? Or simply exhausted from lack of food and sleep?

If she had time, she would have counted five rail lines converging on a couple of platforms. She would have seen the guards and their dogs funnelling the rest of the human cargo out of the cattle cars and onto the cobbled path. Perhaps she could have glimpsed the rooftops of Würzburg stretching away in the distance. But there was little time for her to register anything except what was straight ahead.

She was a prisoner. A slave.

I stood on the cobblestones, looking at what was left of the platforms. Tufts of grass and weeds sprouted where the rails had been ripped out. I could hardly breathe in this place. Even on a sunny day, in a different time, I could feel the terror, the dread Mama and the other slave workers must have felt. They would have been afraid of the guards and their guns. Of being hit and hurt. But the greatest fear must have been the fear of the unknown. What was at the end of the cobblestone path?

I lifted a hand and rubbed an earring. "Oh, Mama," I whispered. I had brought Mama with me on my journey of discovery. I wore her opal and gold earrings, the ones I had bought for her years earlier. The ones she had never taken off. The ones I had slipped from her ears after she died. I had wanted to keep them as a memento of her. And I wanted her with me now.

I had been to Germany a few times as a journalist, but this was different. I was covering my own story, looking for clues that would give me a better understanding of my mother, that would perhaps lead to my birth father, and that I hoped would help me make sense of my own life.

Now, here in this derelict rail yard, I was taking my first steps into Mama's past. Neil and I were guided through this place of past terror by Alex Kraus. I liked him immediately. He was a historian, photographer, author, activist, and, judging by his T-shirt and medallion, a fan of the progressive rock band Magma. He was tall, with a helmet of curly grey hair. He was also part of a group that cemented bronze plaques into sidewalks to remember victims of Nazi atrocities.

Alex hung back as I walked, alone with my thoughts, along the cobblestones. They were slippery, with grass and moss growing between them. I could hear the shuffling of the convoy of new slaves, huddling together for warmth, trudging along under the watchful eyes of the guards. The procession probably would have stopped at the Würzburg Labour Office. There would have been more name-taking and ledger-filling before they were sent off to their new masters. Some were sent to factories. Some to farms.

We hopped into Alex's car to drive to 8 Schillerstrasse, an imposing four-storey building situated on a corner, where Mama worked for Dr. Schroeder, an ear, nose, and throat specialist, and his wife. The exterior was painted yellow-tan and had green vines growing almost to the top floor. Two intricate wrought-iron balconies faced the street on the third and fourth floors.

This had been Mama's new home in Germany. *Not bad*, I thought when I saw it. Before the war, Alex told me, two Jewish families had lived on the top two floors. There was no record of them in the archives. They had either fled or were rounded up and sent to a concentration camp.

I tried to find out who Dr. Horst Schroeder was, but I found no trace of him in the city records. Alex said, "I know of only a few cases of maids, and I believe the employers had to be members of the Nazi party. It was very exclusive to have a maid." Dr. Schroeder must have been useful to the Nazis if they gave him an apartment and a maid.

As I looked at the building with its ornate balcony, I remembered one of the rare times Mama had told me a story about her time in Germany, about how she would cut a slice of bread and then eat it on the balcony while she held the rest of the loaf up to the sun to dry the cut part, to hide the evidence. I burst into tears imagining her hunger. I never felt closer to Mama or felt her presence so strongly as I did there at 8 Schillerstrasse, her first post as an Ostarbeiter.

I got in the car for another short drive, this time to Zeppelinstrasse. Alex parked near a bakery and squinted at a sign. "I can read there *Frauenlandbäckerei*. It's Woman's Land Bakery. This part of the city is called Woman's Land, Frauenland." In the eighteenth century, the area was home to eight convents. The nuns tended vineyards and herb gardens. Now the convents are gone and the area is prime real estate.

The bakery was the same building that was there during the war—large, three storeys, with rose-tinted walls and dormer windows at the top. Mama's friend and cousin Valya Fastykovskaya worked there. I wondered what had become of Valya. Mama seemed to have lost track of her. There were no letters from her after the war. But some digging around in archives revealed that Valya had stayed in Würzburg after the war, married a Russian man, and gave birth to a child in 1945, the first of four.

Schillerstrasse and Zeppelinstrasse were close to Ring

Park, a short walk for Mama and Valya to meet with other slave workers on their days off. Mama had to wear her OST badge, but she could go more or less where she wanted. Despite the war, this was freedom for a seventeen-year-old girl. Mama, Valya, and their friend Lena explored the city and surrounding area, much to the chagrin of their parents. On July 27, 1943, Aniela wrote: *Musya, my dear, if you love me, promise that you will not go to the forest. To stroll in the city is enough, and to sit somewhere in a park. Firstly, you girls do not have all that much time for such a long walk ... you expose yourselves to a big, big danger.*

I imagined Mama met fellow Ostarbeiter Nikolaus Kobetz in Ring Park. Of all the letters Mama left, his is the most intriguing. Nikolaus was twenty-two years old when he wrote to my seventeen-year-old mother on a piece of paper torn from a German company ledger. His Russian penmanship is a work of art. At the end of the letter, he wrote: *P.S. Write a reply and ...* But the rest was obscured by a drawing of a ship floating on a wide smudge of blue ink. I held up the page to the light to see what was behind the smudge and examined it with a magnifying glass. I could make out crossed-out words just before the smudge started, but nothing else.

Did Nikolaus write something, change his mind, and cover it with the ship and the smudge? Or did Mama conceal it? I'll never know. And what did the ship signify? Sailing away from the reality of their lives as slaves?

Nikolaus worked at the Robert Unkel factory, where fat from animal hides was melted down to be used in soap.

It was disgusting, smelly work. But perhaps Nikolaus did clerical work if he was able to get his hands on a page from a ledger.

He only wrote one letter to Mama—or at least, she only kept one letter from him, dated August 17, 1943. He was clearly educated, well read, a young philosopher. *You exist only as workforce for your enemies, while everything else is pushed off to the background; nothing but work; plug your mouth with a chunk of dry bread, don't think of anything above that, because thou art a slave.* But he was angry, frustrated. *Days run by like hours, hours run by like minutes, and this is how months and years lapse, while we are aging, and with aging, the human's happiest season—the youth—goes by, and it does so fruitlessly, without any clear aspirations for a life.* Nikolaus hated his life in Würzburg, and his disdain for the Nazis was apparent. *This is not life, but some kind of existence among these blunt mugs of stone.*

Mama had kept most of her letters in their original envelopes, but there was no envelope for Nikolaus's letter. Nikolaus wrote things that would have landed him and Mama in prison or even gotten them killed if a Nazi censor had read them. He couldn't mail his letter because the Schroeders would certainly have opened it, if the censors didn't see it first. So a friend of his must have passed the letter to Mama. Or maybe Nikolaus slipped the letter into her hand at one of their Sunday meetings. He couldn't speak these thoughts out loud. He knew there were spies everywhere. But, for whatever reason, he wanted Mama to know how he felt. This was a dangerous letter.

How she kept it throughout her time in Germany, and why, is a mystery.

Nikolaus called Mama *Marie*, spelling her name in the French way. But what was he to Mama? She was brought up in a big city: Vinnytsia. Nikolaus came from another big city in Ukraine: Odessa. He was part of the intelligentsia; Mama was part of the bourgeoisie. She loved theatre, music, good restaurants, and dancing. They would have been a good match. Nikolaus suited her temperament and interests. He treated her like a lady, and an adult. Even though Mama was an Ostarbeiter, a housemaid, a slave, she had no parental control for the first time in her life. How did this shape her relationship with Nikolaus? Was he her first love? Was he her lover? It's awkward thinking of Mama that way, but her sexuality was a big factor in her life. Mama liked men—a lot. When I was a teenager it surprised me, at first, when I brought home a boyfriend and she openly flirted with him. As an adult, it embarrassed me when she flirted with men, especially authority figures. She used to call her lung surgeon "my boyfriend" to his face.

I searched for Nikolaus but found nothing. What happened to him? He really is a mystery. I could find no record of him in the Würzburg archives or in the files of the Arolsen Archives on victims of Nazi persecution. But through Nikolaus's letter I see Mama as a young woman with desires, hopes, and dreams. She was beautiful. My friend Eileen once said, "Your mama looks like Elizabeth Taylor."

As we drove around Würzburg, I fell in love with this beautiful Bavarian city tucked into a green valley. It was rich with lavish baroque and rococo architecture. But I learned from archivist Christian Kensy that, just before the war ended, Würzburg was bombed badly. The Royal Air Force dropped incendiary bombs on March 16, 1945. Christian told me, "Everything was destroyed. Fires were hot enough that they sucked in the air from the valley and the fires got hotter." Those fires killed five thousand people and almost obliterated the historic town centre. It destroyed 90 percent of the buildings. All in less than twenty minutes.

Christian showed me a photograph of 8 Schillerstrasse—a blackened shell of four walls. It was providence that Mama wasn't in Würzburg during the bombing.

And what about Nikolaus? Was he reassigned to another city, or did his smart mouth and strong views finally come to the attention of the Nazis? Maybe they killed him. Or maybe he died during the bombing.

Mama missed the bombing because, by then, she had been shipped off to Schweinfurt.

Chapter 22

Schweinfurt

There was no time for Mama to write letters in Schweinfurt. No Sunday outings with friends to explore a new city. No home-cooked meals or a comfy bed in a grand apartment. Mama had been forced to swap her relative freedom in Würzburg for hard labour in Schweinfurt—and a battle for survival.

I had almost no information about Mama's time there, except for a story she would tell. When she was in the workers' camp in Schweinfurt, she and a girlfriend had a rare Sunday off. They managed to get enough hot water so they could have a bath together. As soon as they got into the bath, the Allies began bombing. A guard ran in to order them to leave, but the girls pinched their noses and slipped under the water to avoid detection. The guard fled to the bomb shelter.

Mama and her girlfriend sat washing and watching the skies light up as bombs rained down around them. Their tub shook, the noise was deafening, but Mama told me they didn't care whether they lived or died. Bathing was more important.

I didn't question Mama when she told that story. I merely rolled my eyes because, yet again, Mama was being a drama queen. But it nagged at me. What if the story was true? What if Mama did choose to bathe while bombs fell all around her? I didn't know the depth of her despair, her frustration. I didn't know how exhausted or disheartened she must have been to believe that having a bath was worth dying for.

I didn't know how things we take for granted when they're easily accessible take on such enormous significance when we're deprived of them. We clutch at anything to feel normal. Schweinfurt was such a low point for Mama, she grabbed the opportunity to feel human again, even if it was only a bath that could cost her her life.

I only half believed Mama's bombing story until something unexpected happened. In the early 1990s, just a few years after Neil and I moved to Nova Scotia, Mama and Tata were visiting us and helping us clean up our property. We decided to burn some brush and invite our neighbours to our impromptu bonfire that evening. Our good friends were away for the weekend, but their parents—Russell and Verna Stonehouse—were babysitting their two grandchildren, so we invited the babysitters and the kids to the party. Verna and Russ were Mama and Tata's age, so I thought they would get along.

By 8 p.m. the bonfire was burning bright, flames leaping

high into the sky. The grandkids were running around the fire, while Neil, Verna, Tata, and I were chatting, enjoying a drink, and keeping an eye on the kids. Mama and Russ were sitting in deck chairs on the other side of the bonfire. The flames shot up from time to time, showering us with sparks and lighting up the duo. The kids laughed as they tried to catch the sparks before they died away.

Mama and Russ had only just met, but they were huddled together, deep in conversation, their heads almost touching. A few minutes later, Mama stood up and came hurrying toward me. "He bombed me!" she shouted, giddy with excitement. "When I was in Schweinfurt, he bombed me. Oh my God! Can you believe it? Russ bombed me."

Russ walked up calmly behind Mama. "Well, I guess technically I did bomb your mother. I put those bombs on the planes, and they flew over Schweinfurt. I remember we were bombing day and night." Russ smiled at Mama. "But I had no idea your Mama was there."

"Yeah, yeah, I was in Schweinfurt. At the factories. Can you imagine? Oh my God! He bombed me. Unbelievable!"

They continued smiling at each other, two happy strangers who had just discovered they had a deep connection. Except they were connected by something monstrous.

So Mama's story was true. How true, I didn't know until I went to Germany. Schweinfurt was crucially important to the Nazis. It was, and still is, the ball-bearing capital of Germany. During the war, its four factories produced nearly two-thirds of Germany's ball bearings and roller bearings. All heavy artillery and every tank, plane, boat, truck, machine gun, and submarine needed ball bearings. The factories had to keep producing, day and night. They badly needed workers, but almost all German men were fighting. So the Nazis forced up to 10,000 foreign civilian men and women—slave labourers—to work in Schweinfurt, along with 4,500 prisoners of war.

The factories became prime targets for the Allied forces. They sent waves of bombers, day and night, more than 2,200 planes. The bombings started in earnest in August 1943 and ended in April 1945. Mama was in Schweinfurt by December 1943, just in time for the escalation of the bombing. Mama was at the Kugelfischer factory until July 6, 1944. It was the largest of the four factories in Schweinfurt. Then she was transferred to the SKF factory until March 27, 1945. That was the day when the guards fled the factories in the face of the advancing Allied forces. Afterward, the workers were left to fend for themselves. Mama and the other slave workers searched homes, shops, anywhere to get food. They raided gardens and farms. Sixteen days later, the tanks of the US 42nd Infantry Division—the Rainbow Division—rumbled through the ruins of Schweinfurt and liberated the city.

Neil and I met our guide, Werner Enke, from the Initiative Against Forgetting, a group dedicated to keeping alive the memories and stories of the forced labourers in Schweinfurt. Werner was about my age, a typographer and printer by trade. His short hair was white, and so was his trim beard. He wore a floppy canvas hat and a dark T-shirt, and carried a black shoulder bag filled with papers for our tour. His smile was gentle, his passion for the initiative formidable.

We drove to a large memorial park for the slave workers. It was close to the Autobahn; I could hear the cars whizzing by at insane speeds. The Main River, the longest tributary of the Rhine, bordered the park's grassy fields. On that Sunday in May 2022, I admired the beauty of the place, but my heart felt the pain of what had happened there. This was where Mama became the survivor I had never fully believed she was.

I hoped Werner and his group would help me fill in the blanks of what had happened to her in Schweinfurt. The group painstakingly recorded the experiences of slave workers in the ball-bearing factories. There were seven information boards placed strategically along the path. Werner stopped at each one to talk about the key points and pulled some notes from his bag that expanded on each board's summary. The one that made the biggest impression on me, the one that made me cry, was at a green field dotted with yellow flowers and poppies. It had a quote from an unnamed slave worker after a bombing raid in Schweinfurt: *We ran along the river. The water in the river was red with blood. On the bank lay corpses; often only parts of corpses.*

Barracks used to stand in the field behind that board. Each day, Mama and the other slave workers would have marched 3 kilometres from there to the factory. To my right was the Main River, where so many had died running to find shelter.

I read more stories from former slave workers in Schweinfurt. Mykolaiv Artemenko, taken from central Ukraine, still remembered the horrors of Schweinfurt sixty years later: *The best years of my life at 17 or 18 I had to work and starve under this terrible Hitler regime. The memory is still like this—if I lie down and close my eyes, then I see everything that was then.*

Giovanni Venier, taken from Italy, remembered his first day in Schweinfurt. The guards removed his shoes and forced him to wear clogs. He could barely walk in them. He wore several layers of paper from cement sacks under his clothes to keep warm in winter.

An anonymous Ukrainian forced labourer wrote in a poem: *We go to work in wooden shackles. We come back with tears in our eyes. The legs are sore and bleeding.*

Leonardo Colossi, another Italian, returned to Schweinfurt at eighty-nine for the opening of the Drei Linden (Three Linden Trees) memorial in the park. *Time flies, but I still have vivid memories,* he shared. *I see myself once again fighting the most insidious enemy of all: hunger. I see myself again as a person, ruined, abused, humiliated. I find myself defenceless again, condemned to utter powerlessness against such degradation.*

The Drei Linden memorial was set in a clearing at the end of the walk that led past the former camp and the information boards. Three linden trees stood behind a low semicircular granite monument. A dedication in faded gold leaf ran across the top of the stone. It was the first sentence of the German constitution: *Human dignity is inviolable.* But dignity was a casualty of the war. Fortitude and resilience survived, however; these life-affirming traits certainly endured in my mother throughout her ordeal in Schweinfurt.

Werner, Neil, and I finished our tour at the Drei Linden memorial. Visitors are meant to sit on the memorial. So I did. I gazed directly at the spot where the women's barracks had stood. I remembered Mama's bathtub story and I began to cry. My heart was weighed down with the dark history of the place. The grass in the field was dotted with poppies and spring flowers. Fluffy seed pods were falling gently all around like snowflakes. I watched people walking or riding bicycles, enjoying the warm, sunny day. I wondered if they had any idea of the pain and suffering associated with this place. I wanted to scream at them. I wanted Mama. I wanted to hold her and comfort her. I wanted to tell her she really was a survivor. That I was sorry I had never believed her.

I turned and found Werner, who had stepped respectfully away. We walked to the car, Neil behind us.

"Halina, stop. Look at your shoulder," said Neil softly.

I turned my head slowly. There on my left shoulder was a blue butterfly. I smiled and continued walking. The butterfly stayed with me for quite a while. I knew it was Mama.

Dear Mama,

When I read what happened to you when you were seventeen, I just weep. And I'm so frustrated. Why did you never tell me, Mama? I had to find out through your letters and from my trip to Germany.

Maybe you thought I couldn't handle it? Maybe you wanted to protect me? From what? I don't know. Maybe you were ashamed? Again, of what? None of it was your fault.

At seventeen, your future made a U-turn to hell. I wonder about you as a teenager. What did you dream about before they took you? And did you dare to dream in those dark days during the war? How did you console yourself when those dreams were taken away from you?

At seventeen, my little world was chugging along just great, bursting with opportunities. At seventeen, you were chugging along in a cattle car to Germany.

When I was seventeen, you were thirty-nine. You were

still scrambling to build a life in Canada. Remember how you left Tata and me alone in Sudbury? You went to Southern Ontario to find work. You were living with Margaret and John and their daughters, Eve and Zana. We wrote to each other.

You went from factory to factory, looking for work. You finally got a job at Kralinator Filters Ltd., making filters for jets and cars. You wrote, "I start at 95 cents an hour and after 30 days 5 cents more and bonus. Depends on where they send you to work. Every day different machine. It's not very clean job but I think I stick it for a month or so. I work from 7 to 4 so I have to get up at 5:45. I have 10 minutes to walk."

I'm ashamed of my response: "I'm expecting you to come home on Feb. 14 and no later." It was all about me and a contest for a trip to New York City.

"All the high schools are in this contest and they only pick one winner from the whole city. The trouble with this is, the contest and my Easter exams are all at the same time, so I want you to come home and help me so I can win this trip."

I cringe reading that now, knowing what had happened to you. What different worlds had shaped us ... yours forged in war and violence, mine pampered in peace.

Your education was cut short abruptly. The Nazis finished it for you. They taught you to be a housemaid and a factory worker. So these were the skills you brought to Canada.

I'm so proud you learned to read and write English. Later, those skills helped you get work in two department stores in ladies' wear. You knew about clothes and loved fashion. You were Aniela's daughter, after all.

I had no idea how much you had sacrificed, and how many lies you told in order to survive. I want to hold you and whisper, "It's all right. None of it was your fault."

I'm so sorry I learned all this too late, after you died. Maybe our souls will meet again. Maybe then we'll understand each other more, and love each other better.

Until then, you are still, and will always be, my beautiful Mama.

I love you,

Halina

Chapter 23

Weiden

Weiden was where I fell apart. Right in the middle of the old market square, ringed with cheerfully coloured buildings so typical of Bavarian towns. The buildings, all lit up with twinkly lights, were mostly restaurants and pastry shops popular with tourists. I stood in the square, which had not been touched by the war that shaped my mother's life, and I wept. I was born in Weiden. I felt so connected to this place. I knew I had been here in this square as a baby in my mother's, or my father's, arms. I had stumbled down these cobbled stones as a toddler.

On a soft evening in May 2022 the enormity of Mama's hardships, her pain, and her loneliness broke my heart. I was wearing her earrings. I touched one.

I stood in the square and wept tears of regret and guilt. But I was angry as well. Why would Mama never tell me the terrible things I was discovering as I followed her footsteps? Even now, armed with her letters and my research, I knew only a fraction of her story. Could I have helped her if I had known the secrets she kept? I believed I could. I had no doubt things between us would have been different—if I had been more interested, and she had been less secretive.

I turned and faced an archway at one end of the square. "Did you walk through that archway on your wedding day, Mama?"

Mama had married my father, Stanisław Żebrowski, in Weiden on November 4, 1946. In the middle of the square was City Hall, where they had exchanged their vows.

Were you happy you were marrying Stan? Did you wonder if you were making the right choice? You were six months pregnant with me.

I was sad and frustrated. I had so many questions. Was it too late for answers?

Did Stan help you up those stairs? They're pretty steep. How did you feel on your wedding day? Were you happy? Did you bring me here when I was little? Maybe you bought me an ice cream? Or a pastry? You always loved German tortes and pastries. What kind of life did you have here? Oh Mama, you were only twenty-one.

Weiden archivist Sebastien Schott took me to the city records office and showed me all the documents Mama and Stan signed in order to get married. I felt like I had stepped back in time, knowing my parents had been here signing these papers seventy-six years ago.

Going through them, I made an important discovery. I had no photos of my father. Mama destroyed them all. But here, in the documents he signed in order to get married, were clues to what he looked like. The clerk in the city office recorded his height as five foot nine inches tall, his weight as 150 pounds, and in the space for other features wrote that he had blond hair and blue eyes.

How did Mama get to Weiden? She met Stan in Schweinfurt after the war. At least, that's what she told me once. So how did they get to the La Guardia camp in Weiden? Did they travel together?

Sebastien Schott told me he didn't think the Americans or the UN had organized transport from Schweinfurt to Weiden. So they would have had to make it there under their own steam, just like thousands of other DPs.

If they did, Mama and Stan would have walked at least 145 kilometres. They would have had lots of company: DPs pushing prams filled with household goods, food, everything except babies; DPs pulling carts, or carrying their possessions on their shoulders, all begging for rides, begging for food.

Maybe Mama and Stan caught a rare train running on a set of unbombed tracks. DPs swarmed any surviving train, packing the interior like sardines, hanging from the sides, and perching cross-legged on the roof.

Between May and September 1945, many went home voluntarily. But by the end of September 1945, 1.2 million DPs were milling about Germany, most of them in the American sector, none of them wanting to go back to their countries of origin. Europe was a mess. Journalist W. B. Courtney summed it up in *Collier's* magazine,

July 28, 1945: "Having once seen the wandering lost millions of Europe, you could never forget them, even as you could never fully know what thoughts were in their minds or what lumps were in their hearts. In the rain and wind, they were a steamy, abject porridge of human woe."

By October 17, 1946, UNRAA issued a directive saying that the slogan "Home by Christmas" should appear on all communication in Polish DP camps. They wanted everyone out—and fast. But word had spread about Stalin's retaliation against anyone coming back to their homeland now under Soviet rule. The Poles were definitely not going home for Christmas. They dug in their heels and waited to emigrate.

Somehow in this chaos, Mama and Stan made it to La Guardia. There Mama—Maria Brik—registered as Maria Kotecka, using her mother's maiden name and place of birth in Poland.

My father, Stanisław, became the *barakowy*, the leader of barracks 32, one of the wooden barracks that had housed POWs and forced labourers during the war. The barracks were crudely constructed—cold in the winter, hot in the summer. Mama and Stan created an illusion of privacy by hanging khaki-coloured blankets around their corner of the barracks.

Mama's friends Janina and Henryk also made it to the camp, with their daughter, Jadzia. Mama and Janina lived in drafty barracks, shivering through cold winters where the only warmth came from stolen firewood. They bonded as young mothers struggling to turn the camp rations, heavy on Spam, into child-friendly food.

Jadzia was ten months older than me. We were inseparable until her family moved to America and we went to Canada. Upon arrival, Janina wrote Mama: *As for us, we have already made it to this famous America. May God have mercy on us. Just what kind of life are we going to have here?*

Jadzia's family had encountered their first obstacle as soon as their ship docked: *We were supposed to go to Detroit, but there's unemployment there, and we weren't allowed to go there. They just dropped us at a hotel in New York, and we have to wait until we're given some job.* NCWC [the National Catholic Welfare Council] *is searching, but there is a great lot of people like us, so we've got a lot of waiting ahead of us. I don't know where destiny will take us. For now, we are receiving 6 dollars per family, so that is supposed to be enough. This is how we are pushing our misery down the road*, she lamented. *I don't know how long we are going to suffer like this.*

Janina's family finally settled in Chicago, where Henryk got a job as a maintenance worker for a cemetery. In February 1952, Janina wrote of memories of the camp creeping in: *I recall, time and again, our dreariness, but here it's even stronger. Just work, and nothing else. But I hope that maybe we too will be able to have fun.*

As Janina and Mama adjusted to busy lives in new countries, the letters stopped.

And then, remarkably, in Halifax, when I was seventy-six, I got a call.

"Halinka?" Her voice on the phone was soft, hesitant. The years melted away and I was back in Weiden, playing with my friend.

"Jadzia?"

Within seconds, we were speaking over each other, trying to condense seventy years into one phone call, our hearts flooded with memories. I had contacted her in the US after I found her mother's letters. Our conversation turned to the war. I hoped she could fill in some blanks. I asked her what Janina and Henryk had told her about their days during the war.

"They never talked about it," she replied.

Our parents were typical DPs. They emigrated and kept their mouths shut. They just wanted to forget.

The other person who made it to La Guardia was the man who would become my stepfather, Frank Użarowski. He arrived there, according to camp documents, on November 4, 1946, the same day Mama married Stan. That discovery made me pay attention because I have a letter from Lena, Mama's childhood friend from Vinnytsia, from October 18, 1946, and in the margin she asked, *By the way, where is Frank?*—two and a half weeks before Frank arrived in La Guardia.

Frank was probably at another DP camp in Weiden first—perhaps Fichtenbühl, which housed Poles. Since the DPs were free to move around Weiden, Mama could have met Frank before he was moved to La Guardia with the rest of the Poles in the region.

I wondered if Frank purposely arrived in La Guardia the day Mama got married or if it was just a coincidence. Reading Lena's letter, I sensed she was troubled by Mama's marriage. She asked: *Are you happy with your Stan and with having married him?*

When did Mama and Frank first meet? In Schweinfurt? Were Stan and Mama already together when Frank came on the scene? I don't know. It's a mystery. But what's not a mystery is the profound effect their love triangle had on each other, and on me.

There was yet another mystery in Lena's letter. After the war, Lena had been in Wildflecken, a DP camp in the American zone that was almost a city. Since La Guardia was also in the American zone, it wasn't difficult for her and Mama to write. Later, when Lena contracted tuberculosis, she was transferred to a hospital in Merxhausen, again in the American zone. She was there when she received Mama's letter saying she was marrying Stan and heading for Canada. Lena's six-page reply was a pained stream of consciousness. *Ah, Musin'ka, if you only knew how much anguish I am feeling now,* she wrote, *and how much despair your letter has brought me, despite the word of consolation.*

It's clear their childhood friendship had deepened into a strong bond during their time in Würzburg. But the letter suggests something else, something darker: *Why is fate so unjust?* Lena asked. *Because, you know, I have never done anything evil to anybody. Or, could it be a punishment for what you and I did together and for being compelled twice to breach the oath. But is it possible that nobody, not even God, can understand that we all had to do that; it was forced upon us by destiny?*

I was alarmed. What oath? And why were they forced to break it? Twice? Lena and Mama were only twenty-one years old. What could they have done that was so dire, so dreadful, that not even God could understand? Had they abandoned Valya? There was no mention of her in the letter. Did they have abortions? Did they have sex with Nazis? Or, God forbid, did they inform on someone? Perhaps they broke an oath promising to only marry for love and, instead, got involved with men for protection?

This is another mystery Mama took to her grave. Lena begged Mama to be candid with her: *I want you to tell me the bare truth, because—remember, there was a time in the past, in Würzburg, when you would come to me as if to your mother, with your sorrows and joys.* And, in her role as surrogate mother, Lena warned Mama: *Musin'ka ... preserve your luck for as much as you can, with both your hands and with all your might. (I am hinting here at your character and warning you against any evil, so don't get angry with me.)*

Was Lena referring to Mama's luck getting a man to care for her and her child? Did Lena know Mama had a roving eye and a temper? I don't know if Mama replied, and there were no further letters from Lena.

ONE MYSTERY WAS SOLVED for me in Weiden. I had always thought I was born in the camp itself, but archivist Sebastien Schott showed me proof I was born in a Weiden hospital at 10:30 p.m. on April 10, 1947. Two months later, Mama and Stan took me into town to be baptized at Herz-Jesu-Kirche (Church of the Sacred Heart of Jesus).

I thought I'd been baptized in a small parish church,

but the church is grand. The side chapel with the baptismal is ornate. Herz-Jesu is almost a cathedral. The church administrator showed me the record of my baptism, and I discovered I had a *taufpaten*—a godfather: Leonard Kopecki, a house painter by trade, and another resident of barracks 32 in La Guardia. He was thirty-seven years old and a former POW. Was he a friend of Mama's or Stan's? There are no letters from the man entrusted with my spiritual upbringing. I searched deeper and discovered that two years after Leonard stood with Mama and Stan at the baptismal font, he was on a boat bound for Australia.

Before I left Weiden, I visited the area where the La Guardia camp had stood, where it was home to 1,900 Poles, plus 700 children. I was one of them. The area is now a pleasant subdivision: neat white houses with small emerald lawns.

La Guardia closed on June 11, 1949. The local newspaper reported how decrepit the camp was when the last residents left: "From broken windows, 58 barracks cried out their complete desolation. The barracks, some of which are more than dilapidated, lie empty and abandoned." La Guardia had served its purpose. Most Poles had gone—back to Poland, or to a new life elsewhere. Those who remained were determined to leave Europe, determined to never go back to the USSR.

Weiden had led to discoveries, but in their wake I had more questions: about Mama's secrets, about her oath with Lena, and about the two men in her life. Had she started a relationship with Frank before she married Stan?

From Weiden, Mama, Stan, and I were moved to Bad Reichenhall in Bavaria. Maybe I would find more discoveries, more of the answers I was searching for, in the place the DPs called "Camp Hope."

Dear Tata,

Oh, my heart is heavy now that I understand the depth of your betrayal of my father. You were Stanisław's friend. You even helped him get a visa to Canada, yet you betrayed him. It was all for Mama, wasn't it? You wanted her for yourself. I suppose I can't blame you. She was beautiful, and you fell in love with each other. I was part of the price you paid for loving her.

You brought me up as your own daughter. I never knew until I found my birth certificate that you were not my birth father, but I sensed you were not my blood relative. So I always sided with Mama—my blood.

Mama was a master manipulator. I think you tried to get your side of the story across to me, but Mama got to me first. I wish I had asked you what really happened between you, Mama, and Stanisław.

Before you died, Mama said you were threatening to

throw her out of the house without a penny, and you were going to write me out of your will. I didn't care if you kept me in or not, but I was going to make damn sure Mama got her fair share. See, I always protected her.

I look at pictures of you. You were a handsome man. I can understand why Mama fell for you. That lopsided boyish grin. It was so sweet. And you were so innovative. You could make anything out of anything. And you could certainly talk to anyone. You were just an ordinary miner in Sudbury, yet your best friend was the mayor, Joe Fabbro. He liked you because he could relax with you. You went fishing together. You loved nature.

When Joe died and we went to the wake at his home, I saw you sitting alone, crying. You were heartbroken. You loved him, but you also knew you could get a lot of favours from him. Because of your friendship with the mayor, Mama got her first job at Eaton's department store.

You were manipulative too. You chose people well. You gave them wine, honey, and food because you might need a favour later. Mama was like that too.

And so was I. But now I choose people for who they are, not what they can give me.

Tata, you were an environmentalist, ahead of your time. Weeds were almost sacred to you. I know you pissed off a few neighbours because you never pulled up the dandelions on your lawn. You said the weeds contributed to keeping the earth green.

When you ate papaya—your favourite fruit—you kept the seeds and dried them. When you drove to Florida alone in your van because Mama would no longer go with you, you would scatter the seeds everywhere, like some Polish Johnny Appleseed. I wonder how many papaya trees are growing in Florida now because of you.

I knew how important money was to you, so I never asked you and Mama for money. I paid for my own schooling, my own weddings and homes. Neil and I paid for you and Mama to fly to London, England, when we were there. Yet you gave us a brand-new Toyota when we returned to Canada.

You treated me like your own daughter. Toward the end, before the dementia, you said you loved me. I know you were proud of me. You showed me off whenever you could.

I forgive you for what you did to my father. It was in the name of love. Like Mama and Stan, you were the innocent victim of a war you did not ask for.

I know that you did the best you could for her and for me, your friend's daughter.

I am grateful to you for trying your best to be my father. You did a good job.

I love you,

Halina

Chapter 24

Bad Reichenhall

The more I travelled in Germany, the more deeply I felt Mama's pain, coupled with my guilt for not attempting to understand her better. All the questions I'd had in Weiden swirled around in my head. Camp Hope, on the outskirts of Bad Reichenhall, was my last stop before returning to Canada. My last chance to unravel Mama's past in the country responsible for shaping it. Camp Hope was actually named Camp Tikvah, which translates to "hope" in Hebrew.

I realized Camp Hope was Mama's last hope too. It was her final stop before leaving for Canada. Frank had gone ahead. A few months after we'd arrived in Camp Hope, Stan's visa came through and he, too, left for Canada. For the first time, apart from me, Mama was alone. She knew she would have the responsibilities of being a wife and mother when she got to Canada, but for a brief time she could relax and have a bit of fun. She dressed up and partied with friends. There were trips into town. I have a picture of her smiling in dark sunglasses, striding across a street, looking like one of the movie stars from the glossy magazines she collected so avidly. My beautiful Mama.

During the war, Camp Hope was a Nazi military base, snuggled in the mountains of Bavaria. When the Americans captured it, it became a DP camp, mostly for Jewish concentration camp survivors as well as Polish, Ukrainian, and Baltic DPs. It was one of the biggest camps in southern Germany.

In Camp Hope, everyone was fed and clothed by UNRAA and other relief organizations. For the first time since Schweinfurt, home for Mama was not a drafty wooden barracks. The camp had three-storey buildings and its own administration, hospital, pharmacy, school, synagogue, church, and newspaper, and even a soccer team. At one point, there were about six thousand people there. They were young; they had survived unspeakable horrors, but here, all they had to do was enjoy themselves while they waited for their new lives to begin somewhere else. Somewhere they would not be persecuted or humiliated. At Camp Hope, they could dare to hope, to rest, and to recover, even though they could never forget.

Camp Hope was now Hochstaufen-Kaserne, the Hochstaufen Military Base. I was nervous. Neil and I were going to meet the commanding officer and the city archivist. I thought they might resent talking about Germany's Nazi past.

My anxiety deepened when I saw the German eagle at the entrance to the camp. It was huge, its wings spread open, wrapping around the corner of the building. The eagle held a wreath in the claws that had originally encircled a swastika. The swastika had been sanded off and replaced with the edelweiss, the mountain flower and symbol of Hochstaufen's mountain troops.

I shouldn't have been nervous, though. Lieutenant Colonel Thomas Nockelmann, the base commander, and archivist Dr. Johannes Lang were friendly, open-minded hosts. As we toured the camp, Dr. Lang and I talked about the DPs who had decided to remain in Germany instead of returning home. Both he and the colonel agreed there was a difficult relationship between the DPs and the Germans in Bad Reichenhall.

"Bad Reichenhall was bombed during the last days of the Second World War. It was a horrible bombing." Dr. Lang explained that memories of it lingered when the war was over. "There was a lot of tension between the inhabitants of the DP camp and the population of Bad Reichenhall. In Camp Hope, the DPs had everything they wanted, but in Bad Reichenhall, people were hungry."

Lieutenant Colonel Nockelmann had another perspective on the DPs. "The irony of history is that the DPs were safer in Germany after the war than they would have been in their home countries." If the DPs went home to their Communist countries, they would have been considered traitors. They would need "re-education" to fit in. Many never fit in. They were shamed and shunned by their compatriots even after being in these special camps. Some didn't survive.

I felt a sympathetic bond with Lieutenant Colonel Nockelmann. He empathized with the suffering the DPs and the concentration camps survivors went through. I wondered what he thought about the Nazis. Later, in an exchange of emails, he wrote:

From my perspective I don't feel shame to be a German, but I feel shame about what the Germans have done ... Before my father died in 2017 he told me that my grandfather was an active Nazi member and taught young people about the Nazi doctrines. So, my grandfather was guilty! He supported an inhuman, criminal system responsible for millions of dead people. I cannot make unhappen what has happened, but I can do my part to help to not forget and take responsibility for that not happening again.

Lieutenant Colonel Nockelmann does his part by welcoming survivors and their children to the camp and by sharing the history of the base and the country.

I showed him and Dr. Lang a picture of Mama taken at Camp Hope. She stood almost at attention beside an unidentified man. Mama wore a nice but modest dress, her hair was fashionably styled, and she didn't smile. I notice her feet pressed close, as though she was holding herself together. The man beside her wore a suit but no tie. They looked at something beyond the camera. Both of them—straight, silent, stern witnesses. Looming behind them, the third witness—Hochstaufen Mountain.

"I know exactly where that is," said Lieutenant Colonel

Nockelmann. "It used to be our old parade ground. Now it's a parking lot, but that building in front of the mountain, it's still there. Come."

My heart fluttered. We went to the spot where Mama's picture was taken, probably in 1951. I positioned myself to have my own picture taken in front of the mountain, just like Mama. I held her picture out in front of me.

I burst into tears. I doubled over. I felt some of the fear, the loss, the sorrow Mama had suffered. The kaleidoscope of her life crashed together in my mind. I saw the carefree schoolgirl, the frightened teenage slave worker, the terrified factory worker, the ill-prepared young mother, the troubled wife. In that moment, I loved her more than I ever had before.

I felt guilt at not having made her later years better, for not having worked harder earlier to understand her demons. Standing in Germany, in the exact spot where she had stood seven decades before, I grieved for what could have been.

While Mama was in Camp Hope, she wrote to her parents and sent pictures. There's one of me. I was three years old, standing on a tree stump on the bank of the Saalach River, just across from the camp. I looked anxious, holding my dolly to one side like a prop. I didn't want to be on that stump. What was I doing there anyway? The stump was about two feet high. Who would catch me if I fell off? Where was Mama? Even Aniela commented on it in a letter from March 12, 1950:

Musya, how big and good-looking is Halinka already! I

can't have enough of looking at her! I have covered her photograph with kisses. Such a slender girl. I feel such pity for her, as she stands on a riverbank, all alone on a tree stump, with not a single living soul around her. Of course, I understand that you are nearby, but you can't be seen.

I followed the Saalach River, looking for that tree stump. It was crazy to think I would find it, but I had to look. The banks of the river were overgrown, a tangle of trees, brambles, rocks, and mud, but no tree stumps. Yet I found a spot that gave me an overwhelming sense of having been there before.

That long-ago picture of me on the stump was a metaphor for my life with Mama. I always felt alone. When I needed her most, she wasn't there. And if she was nearby, her drama always came first.

I took care of Mama. I was my mother's mother. Mama never took me in her arms, saying, "Halina, I love you. Halina, you can do anything you want. You're smart. You're wonderful." Mama was incapable of expressing her emotions, but she did tell me once, "My parents spoiled me, and I don't want you to be like me." Maybe withholding love was her way of protecting me.

When I look at the picture of Mama as a five-year-old, standing alone on a chair, her blonde hair cascading out of the bow on her head, I understand why Aniela and Sergei doted on her. She was their golden beauty. So they pampered her. And when she grew up, they continued to infantilize her. They gave her everything they could when she was in Germany, and later in Canada—clothes, food, and family heirlooms. The shipping costs alone would have put a deep dent in their pensions.

Spoiling Mama wasn't their intention, but by their generosity, by treating her like a child, they gave their daughter a blueprint for what she believed was a successful life: Have someone who can give you things, have someone who can take care of you. Sergei and Aniela also unwittingly taught Mama another lesson: Nothing was Mama's fault. So Mama always blamed someone, or life in general, for her miseries. Mama's life was always controlled by someone else: her parents, the Soviets, the Nazis, her husbands, and then me. Plenty of people to blame when things went wrong.

The golden daughter on her chair did her best to raise the girl on the stump. We were two only children posing on our pedestals, one surrounded by love, the other starved of it. Until they died, Aniela and Sergei suffered from the loss of their golden daughter. Aniela especially, as she pleaded with Mama to write to her in March 1950: *Spring has already arrived in our city. Girls are selling the first spring flowers: the snowdrops—remember? The white ones—but I have nobody to buy them for. Perhaps, this is my fate. Oh Musya, how badly do I want to see you! I entreat you, write to me often.* And she wanted to see the granddaughter she knew she could never hold. Aniela wrote on May 1, 1950: *I would give half my life to be able to see Halinka.*

Aniela never did see her granddaughter. And it would be eleven years before she had another letter from her daughter.

I had not expected the memories the camp had dredged up, but, somehow, my tears cleared a block from my heart. As I left Hochstaufen, I felt lighter.

THE NEXT DAY, Neil and I rode up Predigtstuhl on the Grande Dame of the Alps, the oldest gondola in the world. At the top, we walked through the restaurant to the viewing platform. Behind the bar, the bartender, in classic Lederhosen with a Tyrolean hat, was pulling a pint. He noticed us and, without spilling a drop, started belting out the Bruce Springsteen classic "Born in the USA," smiling at us as he sang.

As a proud Canadian, I hate it when people assume I'm American, so without thinking, I sang back, "Born in Bavaria. I was born in Bavaria."

He stopped in mid-pull. "Yeah?"

"Yeah, really. I was born in Weiden ... in Bavaria."

He raised the half-full glass and beamed. "Willkommen!"

I nodded and went out on the viewing deck. I looked at the spectacular mountains in front of me. I looked down at the tiny buildings of the camp below me. I looked at the Germans on the viewing deck around me. And in that moment, despite all the suffering Germany caused the world, despite all the suffering Germany caused Mama, Tata, Stan, and me, I felt a connection to this country. I was, in a small way, part of it.

But more than that, I was able to leave my stamp on Camp Hope. I chatted with Lieutenant Colonel

Nockelmann and archivist Dr. Lang about the existing information boards outside the base. We all agreed the boards could benefit from a makeover.

After I returned to Canada, Lieutenant Colonel Nockelmann contacted me. *Why don't you write something?* he suggested. *If I ask the military to do it, it could take months. The boards need to be changed and I know you can do it faster. Besides, you have a special attachment to this place.*

So I joined forces with Dr. Lang to create new orientation boards telling the story of the barracks and the camp's role in aiding the recovery of so many victims of Nazi inhumanity. True to his word, Lieutenant Colonel Nockelmann had the boards renewed and sent me pictures of the unveiling.

Visitors to the German army barracks in Bad Reichenhall are now greeted with a new sign telling the story of the thousands of displaced people for whom the barracks were a sanctuary of hope after the horrors of World War II. Camp Tikvah was an important turning point in the lives of many DPs. They had escaped the horrors of the Holocaust or their time as slave labourers, and now they had the chance to rebuild their lives.

I am proud beyond words to have been part of a project that will help future generations understand the importance of the place we called Camp Hope.

Chapter 25

Hopes and Dreams

Among Mama's documents was a faded yellow brochure—folded to fit easily in a business envelope. It was Mama and Tata's only advertising for their Killarney Island Lodge, apart from word of mouth. There was a picture on the cover of the living room and fireplace in the old white clapboard house. The brochure extended an invitation to potential visitors:

Imagine a peaceful old world fishing village—a jewel of a spot nestling around a snug harbour with towering mountains and primeval forest as a backdrop—that is Killarney. And now for the first time one can drive to the isolated spot on a newly constructed Government Highway, carved through the wilderness past scenery unsurpassed in the Sudbury District. There one can find complete relaxation and recreation, so vital to the keyed up nerves and tired bodies of business men and women. Cool nights and pleasant days.

All of this could be enjoyed for just eight dollars per

person, per day—that included a room and all meals—and it required only a ten-dollar deposit to secure a reservation. Black-and-white pictures showed people fishing and a hunter with a dead deer at his feet. And at the bottom, a signoff from *Your host, Frank Uzaroski*. They managed to misspell his name.

The brochure made me sad. It was amateurish, even by advertising standards then. I'm sure Tata had it done on the cheap.

Yet, for me, Killarney has always remained a special place. In 2015, when I was sixty-eight, I was drawn back. I had to see my white clapboard house one more time. It was, after all, the first real house where Mama, Tata, and I lived. And it was the first place where Mama had been really happy. She would be alone at the lodge in the spring and fall while I went to school and Tata was still working in the mine in Sudbury.

Sadly, in 1970, Mama and Tata sold the Killarney Island Lodge, their final failed business venture. I'd heard there'd been a fire, but I wasn't prepared for what I found when I returned. I borrowed a canoe and paddled across the narrow channel to our old dock. As I got close, I could see the top of the chimney. I pulled the canoe onto the beach and climbed the hill to the house, but the house was gone. The chimney and the fireplace were all that remained. But the fireplace was still erect and straight, a monument to resilience. I wept as I stood before my old friend. I had dried my hair in front of its roaring fire, read books by its light. I had been mesmerized for hours by the red, orange, and yellow flames dancing over the logs. I had loved that fireplace. It comforted me when I was alone in the house. Now, here it was, alone, exposed to the elements, reduced to a campfire pit for tourists.

I placed my hands on its rock. "I'm still standing too." I wanted to comfort it as it had comforted me. "You were such a beauty," I whispered, as I caressed the stones.

But the fireplace didn't need my pity. There was an aura of dignity about it still. It was a survivor. It used to be the focal point of a quaint house; now, it stood alone in the wilderness. The land around it had been bought by the Sportsman's Inn across the channel, and the staff had put benches around the fireplace. It still had a purpose. It warmed the tourists and toasted their marshmallows. This was just another phase in its existence. Its world had changed, but the old fireplace still stood and served.

That day, I realized I was just like my fireplace. I had survived much. I had walked away from a plane crash when I was covering the 1988 Canadian elections, dodged bullets in the Romanian Revolution, gotten out of Baghdad hours before the Allies bombed it in the Gulf War. I'd left the world of journalism behind, set up a successful business as a speaker and performance skills coach. Now I was a writer. My life was evolving, my focus shifting, my purpose changing, but I still had a role to play.

I looked again at my fireplace, still standing tall and proud, and I wept, not because I was sad but because it inspired me. If it could stand, after everything, so could I.

In the Killarney of 2015, I saw what Tata had dreamed of but never known how to capture. I saw docks that hadn't been there in 1965 when Mama and Tata bought the property. I saw boats and yachts of all sizes moored at those docks. I saw boat traffic in the channel. In the village, new restaurants were frying, sautéing, and baking up a storm to feed a constant influx of tourists. Tata had been right. The road to Killarney changed everything. Had he and Mama known how to promote and manage a business, they could have been rich.

But even more significantly, something magical had happened to me in that house.

It was a Saturday at the end of April in 1965. Mama, Tata, and I were in Killarney, preparing for the summer season. Tata was puttering in the boathouse, and Mama was making breakfast in the kitchen-dining room when I rushed in.

"Mama, I saw something."

Mama didn't look up from the porridge she was stirring on the stove. "What?"

"When I woke up, there was a woman standing at the foot of my bed."

"A woman?"

"Yes."

"Ach, Halina, you were still sleeping. You were probably dreaming."

"No! I was awake, Mama. She was wearing a wide-brimmed hat. It was black. And she had a long black coat with a fur collar. Her clothes were really old-fashioned.

She just stood there and looked at me. She was beautiful, but she seemed really sad."

Mama stopped stirring the porridge. "A wide-brimmed hat and a black coat? With a fur collar?"

"Yeah. It was weird. She wasn't scary. I wasn't afraid. She was just there when I woke up, just looking at me. And then she was gone."

Mama stood still, the porridge bubbling hard in the pot. She gazed vacantly at the kitchen shelves.

"Mama!"

I grabbed the wooden spoon and saved the porridge. Mama didn't even notice. She went into the dining room and looked out the window at the church across the channel. I followed, stood in the doorway, and stared at her back. She gazed out the window, lost in thought for a long time. It was clear, for the moment at least, that her world had closed around her and she didn't want to talk.

Mama never did speak to me about that moment. It was only after I found her letters that I started putting things together. I found some photographs among her papers—there was Aniela, buttoned up to the neck in a winter coat with a fur collar and wearing a wide-brimmed hat. Aniela had died in Vinnytsia, just a couple of weeks before I burst into the kitchen with my news. Mama would have known Aniela was seriously ill, though Sergei had not yet told her of her death.

Did Mama have a premonition? I think she was already grieving for her mother, and my vision confirmed her worst fears.

But why did Aniela's ghost visit me? I carry the hope that Aniela came to see me—her Halinochka, her only grandchild whom she loved all her life—because she knew she could never hold me, never give me bouquets of spring flowers like she did Mama, and never spoil me. An ocean, a repressive ideology, and her failing health separated us forever. But I have never forgotten that vision of my grandmother, my *babcia*, watching me at the foot of my bed. It's as clear today as the day I saw her in 1965.

Dear Grandma Aniela,

I cherished that line in your letter—"I would give half my life to see Halinka." Oh Grandma, I would have given half my life, too, to see you, to have you hold me, spoil me, and give me spring flowers. But we weren't meant to meet in person.

Yet I saw you, once, a vision, standing at the foot of my bed. When I look at your photograph in the wide-brimmed hat and the coat buttoned up to your neck, I know it was you. I am so happy you came to see me.

I often think you, Mama, and I are like a matryoshka doll—you know, those cheerful Russian nesting dolls. Except there's nothing cheerful in our stories.

You're the first and biggest matryoshka, Grandma. I name you Despair. You lost your golden daughter on what you called "that accursed day," and you never saw her again. You blamed yourself for the rest of your life, for something you could not have prevented.

Mama is the second matryoshka. I call her Deception. She was an innocent girl when the Nazis took her. To survive, she did whatever she had to do to stay alive. She built such an intricate web of lies, they entangled her for the rest of her life.

The final matryoshka is me. I'm Discovery. I'm the last of our little threesome. There is no other matryoshka doll after me. I set out to discover who I am, but I could only do this by understanding what happened to you and Mama.

Oh, Grandma, Mama kept secrets from you, and from me. I think she was afraid you'd be disappointed in how her life turned out—the horrors she endured in Germany and the hardships in Canada. You and my grandfather worked so hard to give her everything. She couldn't disappoint you by telling you the truth.

Mama lied and kept secrets from me too. I live haunted by them, trying to untangle them.

It hurts me so much that we never met, Grandma. Yet I feel your presence when I hold your letters, or touch the napkins you embroidered, or brush my hand on the golden velvet tablecloth you sent us, or see my reflection in the samovar on our dining room buffet.

You are everywhere in my house. You are in my heart. I will always remember you.

Your loving granddaughter,

Halinka

Chapter 26

Damn Polacks

By the time I was five, I knew that being called a DP was bad. Once, when Mama and I went to the butcher in Sudbury, the owner muttered "Damn DP Polacks" just loud enough for us to hear as we were leaving. So I understood DPs were bad people, unwanted people, and I was one.

But I didn't know what I, or Mama, or Tata, or any of the DPs in Sudbury had done that was so bad that many Canadians, French and English, called us by this name. It was like they were spitting on us.

Why didn't they like us? Was it our accent, as we tried to speak English? Was it our food—those strange-sounding dishes like pierogi, borscht, and kielbasa? Did we look different? We were just trying to fit in. We just wanted to live normal lives.

I hated being a DP. Even if, in those early years in Sudbury, I didn't know what it meant. I learned that being a DP meant you'd lost everything—your home, your family, and possibly your country. Being a DP meant your life had gone to hell, your loved ones were probably dead, and there wasn't a single damn thing you could do about it. Being a DP meant you had committed the ultimate sin of not only being in the wrong place at the wrong time, but also of being the wrong kind of person, an outsider. And because of that, you were destined to suffer.

Slowly, I realized that, in the eyes of many Canadians, a DP was a loser, a scrounger, someone looking for an easy ride to prosperity on the backs of hardworking folks who didn't have strange accents or unpronounceable names. So after we emigrated, we kept our mouths shut.

I didn't want to be a DP. Unfortunately, my name—Halina Żebrowska—gave me away. So in grade four, without consulting anyone, I changed Halina to Helen. As long as no one asked for my full name, I could pretend I was Canadian.

I made a point of having Canadian playmates. It wasn't easy in my early school days, when I spoke little English. Mama tried to make me take Polish lessons—no way; I was going to be Canadian and speak perfect English. Much later, I regretted not studying Polish.

One summer's day when I was six years old, I was hanging around the boarding house, bored and getting in everyone's way.

"Ach, Halina. Look," Mama said, pointing to a row of twelve empty lunch pails. "I have to pack all these for the night shift. Go play with your friends."

"I don't have any friends," I pouted.

School was over. It had been hard to make friends, learn a new language and new customs, and go to school for the first time.

Mama shooed me outside. I stood on the sidewalk. It was hot and bright. I squinted and saw a little girl across the street. She looked Canadian.

"Wanna play?" I shouted.

"Okay!" she shouted back, in perfect English.

No accent! I ran across the street. "Hi, I'm Halina."

"I'm Eileen. How old are you?"

"I'm six."

"I'm seven. I go to St. Thomas school."

"I go to Prince Charles. Do you have any brothers or sisters?"

"No. Do you?"

"No. What's your last name?"

"Maizuk," said my new friend.

I was astonished. Her last name didn't sound very Canadian. "What kind of name is that?" I asked.

"Ukrainian."

"Ukrainian! I thought you were Canadian."

"I am. I was born in Sudbury. And my mother and my father were too. But my baba came from the old country. Are you Ukrainian?"

"No. Polish. We just moved here."

"Okay. Let's go play."

And so began a friendship that has lasted a lifetime. Eileen was skinny, taller than me, with fine, dark-brown hair and warm brown eyes. I liked her immediately. She was a Canadian, but she understood my DP world. Bonus!

She became my best friend, my refuge during those hectic years growing up in Sudbury—and later. We lived around the corner from each other, me in my tar-papered shack, Eileen in a modest grey stucco house.

Our neighbourhood was spilling over with DPs—Poles, Ukrainians, Germans, Russians, and Jews from all over Europe. Even though Mama didn't talk about her war experiences, other DPs did. As children, Eileen and I heard stories told in quiet voices by grim-faced adults, nodding their heads, sighing, "Ach. So terrible. Unbelievable." We didn't understand the stories, or why the talking always stopped when we entered the room, but we heard enough to be intrigued.

One summer, when we were about eight or nine, we created a new game. We called it "concentration camp." We would bring a jar of water and some old spoons to Eileen's parents' garage. It was empty most days, as Eileen's father drove the family car to work. After we closed the doors, it became our "concentration camp." We planned our escape in whispers. We needed food and water. We opened the door a smidge every few minutes to make sure there were no guards around. When the coast was clear, we crept outside to the side of the garage, shushing each other along the way.

Eileen's mother had rhubarb plants there. We broke off some large leaves, hid them under our shirts, and sneaked back to our garage prison. The guards never noticed we were gone. In the dim light, we scraped a hole in the garage's dirt floor with our spoons, splashed in some water, and made mud. We stuffed the mud into the rhubarb leaves, rolling them up like cabbage rolls, just the way we had seen our mothers do. When the coast was clear, we made our escape and ran for the woods behind the garage. We rested smug in our victory over the guards. Our reward was to pretend-eat our cabbage rolls.

At the time, I never felt this was an odd game. Didn't all children play concentration camp? Eileen and I understood that concentration camps must have been very bad from the way the adults talked about them. We knew nobody wanted to be in one. But we didn't know why, and nobody told us. Now, I'm mortified. Now, I know the only escape from a concentration camp, for so many, was death.

I forgot about the concentration camp game until my early teens. One day, I was bored and rummaging aimlessly in Mama's bedroom drawers, a favourite distraction of mine. I found a tattered envelope well hidden under her scarves. There were three pictures inside.

The first was just four inches by two and a half. A pile of corpses, partially clothed, their heads shaved, mouths open, all thrown carelessly one on top of the other. A small snapshot of the massive barbarity of the Nazis. In the middle was the body of a girl. Unlike the others, her head was not shaved and she was wearing clothes. I stared at her. I felt I knew her. She looked peaceful, a sleeping angel.

The second picture was of three men in striped clothes. They were balancing a wooden plank between them, getting ready to push it into a crematorium oven. There was a naked male body on the plank. The dead man faced the camera as well.

The third picture was of three long gallows in the woods. I counted eleven bodies hanging from them.

I asked Mama about the pictures. "Ach, they're from the war," she said and snatched them away from me. The pictures went back into the drawer. She never talked about them again. I never forgot them.

Years later, I learned the truth about concentration camps. I asked Mama if she was ever in one. "No!" was all she said.

I discovered that American soldiers were distributing these photos after the end of the war. They wanted the world to know the horrors they had seen when they entered the camps.

How did Mama get these photos? Probably from a GI. The question that nags at me is why she kept them. Did she want a reminder of what she had escaped? Did she keep them to show others? To show me?

When I look back at those years in Sudbury, what I remember is the resilience of most of the DPs. They had little or nothing, except a determination to make a new start and a willingness to work. But not everyone was this keen. Some were so scarred by the war that they went about their new lives as though on automatic pilot, not caring if they were successful or not. They just wanted regular food on the table and no bombs when they ate it. The DPs faced prejudice and discrimination, but that was nothing new; they had been humiliated by the Nazis, called subhuman, and they had survived that. Being called a DP was nothing.

Life was not always a bed of roses in their new countries. When they emigrated, the biggest piece of baggage many carried was their demons. Today we would diagnose many of the DPs with PTSD. But back then nobody talked about post-traumatic stress disorder. Everyone was expected to "get a grip" on their emotional baggage, to be grateful for their new lives, and to just get on with them, no matter what names people called them. So most DPs just kept their mouths shut and suffered in silence. A few told their stories, but Mama and Tata weren't among them. They struggled on with little help and less understanding. As a result, their demons defined their lives—and mine.

Once, when I was seven, Mama, Tata, and I went for a picnic by a river. The three of us walked to a grassy spot away from the highway, and Mama laid a blanket by the riverbank.

"Here, Halina, sit down and stay here. We'll be back soon. Be a good girl."

"Where are you going, Mama?"

"Oh, Tata and I just need to see something over there." Mama made a vague gesture toward the woods. "We'll be back soon. Look, there are some pretty irises by the river."

As she said this, Mama removed a second blanket from a bag and smiled at Tata. He grinned back and took her hand, and they disappeared into the trees.

I sat very still, looking at a cow chewing placidly on

the other side of the river. Could it swim across and attack me? It wasn't a very wide river. I was scared. Scared to be alone in these woods that I didn't know. Scared Mama and Tata wouldn't come back. Too scared to cry.

As an adult, I realized they were making love in the woods while I waited, terrified, without moving a muscle.

I was left alone a lot. Mama and Tata went on vacation once for a few days and left me under the supervision of our landlady. I went to school, ate at the boarding house, and slept in the rooming house.

In the beginning, Mama and Tata were passionately in love. There wasn't room for me. They had lost their youth to a brutal war. They never knew what it was to be young and free. Each day had been a matter of life and death that required all their energy to survive. They just wanted to recoup what they'd lost, have fun, and, yes, make money.

Their behaviour left emotional scars on me that took years and many therapists to heal. I've carried a sense of abandonment most of my life. But the scar of being abandoned on the riverbank was nothing compared to the scar I acquired one summer night when I was ten years old.

Tata was working night shift at the mine, and Mama was working night shift too, filling lunch pails at the boarding house. Whenever they left me alone at night, which was often, at a time when hiring a babysitter was unheard of, they padlocked the shack door from the outside. That night was warm, so they left their bedroom window open.

I was dreaming I was lying on the beach with my friend Judy. In my dream, she rolled over and lay on top of me. I couldn't breathe. I couldn't get her off me.

Suddenly, I woke up. Someone really was in bed on top of me. I turned on my bedside lamp. A hand reached out and turned it off, but not before I saw his face. It was Johnny, one of the men from the boarding house! I screamed.

He put his hand over my mouth. "Shhh. It's okay."

I tried to scream again. I couldn't. I tried to wiggle away. I couldn't. His weight smothered me.

"Shhh. It's okay." His hand reached under the covers. His fingers slid into my pyjamas. He began massaging me. He put his finger inside me. His other hand was tight on my mouth. I couldn't move. He was breathing heavily into my neck.

After a while, he took his hand from my pyjamas. He shifted his weight. I heard a zipper. "Shhh. Don't be afraid. Here, touch here." He guided my hand to something long, hard, and moist. "Shhhh. It's okay. Be quiet now. Everything's all right." He was still breathing hard. Then he rolled off and left.

I lay very still until I was certain he had left. Then I turned on my light and looked around my room. Nobody. The shack was quiet.

I put my sneakers on and ran to the porch, to a small window with a bench underneath. I stood on the bench and opened the window wide enough to crawl through. I raced down the dark, empty streets, my heart pounding, flung open the boarding house door, and charged into the dining room like all the demons in hell were chasing me.

"Mama! Mama!"

"Halina!" Mama dropped the sandwich she was putting into a lunch pail. "Halina! What are you doing here? What's wrong?"

"Johnny was in bed with me, Mama." I was in my pyjamas and sneakers, my hair plastered to my face.

Two women came out of the kitchen. A couple of men who were going to work rose from the dining table.

"Johnny?! Johnny was in your bed?"

"Yes, Mama. Johnny." I started to cry.

Mama, the women, and the men all looked at me as though I had two heads. Everyone liked Johnny. So did I. He was funny. He told a lot of jokes, and people enjoyed playing jokes on him.

Someone called the police. Mama took me home. The next day, Mama, Tata, and I went to the police station.

"You said Johnny touched you?" the detective asked gently.

I nodded.

"Where did he touch you?"

I cringed. I looked at Mama and Tata. I didn't want to answer. I stood there, burning with shame. Finally, I pointed to my crotch. Was it bad to be touched down there? I wanted Mama or Tata to explain what had happened. What was so important about "down there"? What taboo had Johnny violated because he touched me there?

Neither Mama nor Tata explained anything. Mama was incapable of dealing with my emotions. She would never have known how to speak to a child about the facts of life. Aniela and Sergei probably never told her.

I'm positive they would never have reported the incident if someone in the boarding house hadn't called the police. Mama and Tata both had a healthy fear of the law. They were recent immigrants. They were unwed. Mama had lied about her identity to get to Canada. They didn't want to rock the boat.

A few days later, Johnny's friend approached me while I was playing in front of the boarding house. "Why did you say those bad things about Johnny?" he demanded.

The man was a stranger. I was scared.

"You know you ruined Johnny's life, don't you? Why did you lie?"

"I didn't lie!"

I ran into the boarding house and hid in the storeroom. I sat on the floor next to a sack of potatoes and rocked myself. Did Mama and Tata believe me? Did the police believe me? Did anyone believe me?

One of the men in the rooming house next door believed me. His bedroom window faced our shack. He said he had heard a scream that night.

Johnny disappeared from the boarding house and the community. I never knew what happened to him, and I didn't care. I became the talk of the neighbourhood. People stared at me. Mothers told their children not to play with me.

Only my best friend, Eileen, stood by me. "My father said if that had happened to me, he would have killed the man."

Why didn't Tata kill Johnny? Didn't Tata love me enough to defend me? I was an object of curiosity and pity for a long time. I was ashamed. Surely I had done something wrong to drive Johnny to do what he did.

It was another year before Mama raised the subject again, when I was eleven years old. I was doing homework at the kitchen table in the shack. Mama came in and put a magazine on the table: *True Confessions.*

"Halina, you know this magazine?"

"Yeah."

"They got good stories here. I betcha people get paid lots of money for them."

"I guess."

"I think you should write your story for them."

"What story?"

"You know, about Johnny. We can get some money. Buy some nice clothes."

I looked at Mama, stunned. She wanted me to write about what happened? All I wanted to do was forget about it. Forever.

"No! I'm not going to write about that. No!"

"Halina, just listen to me. We can get good money. Don't you want pretty things? And you can change your name and his, if that's bothering you. Nobody would know. Okay? Be a good girl and do what Mama says."

"No!"

It was only much later that the full impact of what Mama had been asking me to do hit me. My own mother wanted to use my trauma to benefit herself. What really hurt was that she didn't think it was wrong.

It was more proof of how emotionally removed she was from me. I was always learning that Mama thought only about Mama. It would never have occurred to her to consider how her secrets, her decisions, her actions, might affect me.

The biggest secret she kept from me was my birth father, Stan. She could only think of him in relation to herself. He was the man who abused her. She couldn't understand how not knowing about him might affect me.

I had endless sessions with therapists to deal with issues of abandonment and loneliness. I felt unworthy of love. It affected my relationships. If my father couldn't love me by coming back for me, how could any man love me?

The more I thought about him, the angrier I got. Stan was a jerk for leaving me. He was an even bigger jerk for not coming back to find me. Who was he? Why did his relationship with Mama sour? What happened to him? Much of my life, it seems, has been overshadowed by a man I barely knew.

Chapter 27

The Man in the Chateau

I slammed into my father's chest, almost crushing my toy stove and throwing him slightly backward. I was so excited! The kind of crazy excited only a four-year-old can get when Santa has just given her the best present ever. My father was on bended knee, his arms catching me as I squealed across the wooden floor.

"Oop-la," he laughed, scooping me up and then standing without disturbing the precious stove I was clutching. He feigned great interest as I showed him how to open and close the little oven door, and how to pretend to turn the tiny stationary knobs on the front.

This is the only memory I have of my father, Stanisław Żebrowski. It was my first Christmas in Canada. We were in either a church or a union hall. I can't remember which, but I know we were in Timmins, Ontario.

And it's not much of a memory of my father—I couldn't take my eyes off my stove to pay real attention to him. So my memory is a feeling, a sensation of total happiness and contentment in the arms of a faceless man.

Ten months later, Mama left Stan and took me with her. We went with Frank Użarowski to Sudbury, Ontario. I forgot Stan. Frank became my Tata, my dad.

Years later, when I was an adult, usually at Christmas, I would dust off that memory of my little stove and my father. I tried so hard to remember his face, but I just couldn't. I finally started searching for him in earnest in my seventies. I didn't want to die without knowing who he was and what he looked like.

One day in October 2022, Neil called from his office upstairs, "Halina, have you ever heard of findagrave.com?"

"No, why?"

"I think I've found Stan."

It was that easy. A website. Something we never investigated because we were so focused on following Mama's footsteps in Germany. Once we were back in Canada, the focus shifted to finding my father.

I had already searched for him in my twenties, and again in my fifties, and failed both times because there was never enough accessible information. The digital age made all the difference. From the camp documents, I knew my father's date and place of birth. Now we had solid data to plug into online search engines.

We had already found a census record for 1972 of a Stanisław Żebrowski in Kirkland Lake, Ontario. More research revealed he had been in a nursing home there on Chateau Drive.

"There's a Stanisław Żebrowski buried in a cemetery in Kirkland Lake," Neil said.

I ran up the stairs to his office, my heart beating.

"Kirkland Lake is close to Timmins. Mama thought Stan might have gone back to Poland, but what if he didn't?" I mused. "What if he stayed up north? Kirkland Lake is a small town. How many Stanisław Żebrowskis could there be in that cemetery who were the right age and were born in Nienalty, Poland?"

"I think we've got our guy," said Neil.

"I think so too." I sat in the chair, absorbing the information that had eluded me for so long. Could it really be him? It had to be.

My father. I'd finally found him.

After a call to the cemetery manager, Dave Pearce, to confirm what we had seen online, it was time for a road trip to the small mining community of Kirkland Lake. We drove for three days from Halifax and arrived at the Swastika Cemetery on the outskirts of town. The irony of the name of the graveyard was not lost on us. Kirkland Lake shared the cemetery with the village of Swastika, a few kilometres away. Swastika was the name of the community long before the Nazis desecrated the ancient symbol of prosperity and good fortune.

"Stanisław Żebrowski is buried in an unmarked grave," said Dave. "Plot 17, section 13. Says here he was sixty-four when he died. I'll take you up there."

I was so close I could almost feel my father reaching out to me. We stopped on top of a hill. All around, for as far as I could see, were gravestones and long swaths of lawn waiting for future inhabitants. Bordering the graveyard was a forest of evergreens standing guard like soldiers ensuring the dead could rest in peace. I can't remember if it was quiet there or not. I don't remember hearing anything—no wind, no birds, no traffic, just the thumping of my heart.

We walked between rows of gravestones, some elaborate, some simple, some with flowers, some looking forgotten, all chronicling lives lived. Dave stopped at a space between two headstones, in front of a patch of bare grass.

"I put a marker for you," he said.

I walked to it, clutching a bouquet of flowers and a keychain with a small silver heart. I knelt on the grass. The marker was like something you would see in a grocery store naming fruits or vegetables and their price. Cherries, $1.50/lb. Only here, the tiny metal stake held a small piece of paper with ZEBROWSKI written on it. The paper was secured to the metal with clear adhesive tape.

All the anger I felt toward my father for never coming for me when I was a child melted away. I reached for the marker and held it tight. I wept. I wept because this was the closest I would ever get to him. I wept because, deep down in my heart, I knew he was just as much a victim of the war as Mama. His life was stolen, just like hers. I wept because, whatever had happened, he didn't deserve to lie unmarked and unmourned in the Swastika Cemetery.

"Do you remember me, Stan? It's Halina, your daughter." I sobbed. "I don't know what to call you. Frank was my tata ever since I was four years old. I'm used to calling him Tata, so if you don't mind, I'll call you Stan. I'm so happy I found you. I've been looking for you for a long time, Stan. Mama never told me much about you and your life with her, but she said awful things about you. She said you treated her badly and that's why she had to run away from you. She died, you know. And so did Frank. I'm the only one left. I'm sorry it took so long for me to find you. But, you know, the important thing is that I did. And the first thing I'm going to do is get a proper gravestone for you."

I draped the keychain heart on the marker. I wanted to give him something, anything, to show I cared. I arranged the flowers in front of it. I visited his grave every day until we left.

On the last visit, I told him: "I'm not going to cry. I'm done crying. I want you to know I love you. No matter what happened in the past, you are my father. But I need to ask you one thing that still hurts me so much. Why, oh why, did you never come looking for me after Mama left you? Was I such a bad girl you didn't want me anymore? Oh, Stan, I used to feel so guilty because of that. And unwanted. And then I got really mad. I thought you were an asshole for never coming for me. Who did you think you were? A father doesn't abandon his child, his little four-year-old daughter, for God's sake, does he? Well, you did—or maybe you didn't. I don't know for sure. Maybe you did try looking for me and couldn't find me. Either way, it doesn't matter now. I found you.

"I was in therapy for years dealing with abandonment

issues. I always thought that love meant someone would leave me. I was really screwed up for a long time. But now that I understand what happened to Mama, I know your life was shattered too because of the war. So I don't blame you anymore. I do love you. I always remember how you held me that Christmas when I got my little stove. Do you remember? We were so happy together. A perfect father and daughter. You will always be my father, Stan. I'll be back to see you again soon. You will never be forgotten. Please rest in peace."

It was a bittersweet moment. Yes, I had finally found my father's resting place, but I still didn't know anything about him. I didn't know what he looked like. I didn't know what kind of man he was.

Dave gave me a burial certificate with the name of the funeral home. I went there and got Stan's statement of death. He died of a stroke on April 2, 1978. He was penniless. The city paid $700 for his burial. His body was placed in the underground vault at the cemetery because the ground was too frozen for a grave to be dug. Stan was buried on May 27, 1978, with no one present.

Later, I got Stan's full death certificate from the Ontario government. A coroner wrote that he'd had a previous stroke when he was about fifty-seven that had left him with paralysis on his right side.

His occupation was listed as a bush worker in the timber industry. His marital status at the time of his death was unknown, but *Nadia, surname unknown* was listed under *Name of wife*. Who was this mysterious Nadia? I hoped Stan had a companion after Mama and I left him. Finding Stan was already leading to more questions than answers.

But one piece of the puzzle of my mother's life did fall into place as I studied my father's death certificate. Among Mama's papers, I had found a certificate of her marriage to Tata. They had married in secret in November 1978. They told no one, not even me.

Now I had a document in my hand saying my birth father had died in April 1978. Could it be a coincidence that just a few months after Stan died, Mama and Tata—who had been living as husband and wife for twenty-five years—got married, not in Sudbury among friends, but in a civil ceremony in North Bay, an hour and a half away, with no one in attendance?

Whenever I asked Mama about Stan, she always said she didn't know if he was dead or alive, didn't know where he was, and didn't care. But after a quarter of a century of living unwed with Tata, she decided to marry—a few months after Stan died. It was too much of a coincidence. Someone must have told Mama that Stan was dead. Otherwise, how could she have known she was free to remarry? Had she or Tata, or both of them, been keeping tabs on Stan ever since they left him?

If they had, then Mama had lied to me during the fight I'd had with her when I was in my fifties, when I was trying to find him. I had asked her if she knew where he was. She'd said no, he probably went back to Poland. But she knew all along he was still in Canada.

Mama was fifty-three when Stan died. I imagine the choice she might have faced—marry Frank and get him to make an honest woman out of her, or leave Frank for a life of her own. I know she stayed with Frank because, as the old saying goes, better the devil you know than the devil you don't know. No matter how hard I tried to convince her that her life would be better without Tata, Mama would never leave him.

I was thirty-one when my birth father died. I still knew nothing about him, and Mama didn't volunteer any information. But in my fifties, when I began searching for him, she opened up a bit. I think it was because Stan was dead and she felt safe in the eyes of the law. So that's when she told me about Stan abusing her.

Stan died at the Chateau Nursing Home in Kirkland Lake. I have no idea how he got there. Perhaps through his logging employer. The Chateau was once the grand home of Sir Harry Oakes, an American who discovered gold in Kirkland Lake, retired to an estate in the Bahamas, and was murdered there in 1943. The Chateau became a small nursing home in 1967. When I visited in 2022 it was a museum.

The two-storey building was built of logs and painted a cheery yellow. It had a large wraparound veranda. Did Stan sit there and look at the tree-lined street? I wandered the rooms, imagining Stan there. Each room I went into, I thought I caught a glimpse of him—a faceless old man leaning on a cane, or perhaps in a wheelchair, looking out the window. I felt his presence everywhere, and it comforted me. The Chateau Nursing Home was small. Stan must have had good care and attention there. I was glad his last days were in this elegant, comfortable log house.

WHEN NEIL AND I got back to Halifax, I put a plea on Facebook asking if anyone knew a Stanisław Żebrowski at the Chateau Nursing Home in the 1970s.

Sonia Pietrasik-Lang answered. She was a young nurse's aide at the Chateau in the 1970s. She nursed my father in the last years of his life. She wrote: *I remember your dad very well. What I remember is he was paralyzed on his right side, possibly from a prior stroke. His arm was totally paralyzed and his leg was affected as well—although he walked with a cane.*

Sonia said Stan spoke Polish when he wanted something and kept to himself. After all his years in Canada, he still didn't speak English. But then again, all his friends were DPs, so there was no urgency to learn another language. Stan shared a room with two French-Canadian men. They spoke little English; Stan spoke no French. Yet, Sonia said, they all got along. Their common bond was smoking and sitting looking out the window of their room, or on the veranda when the weather was good. She wrote: *Your dad took pride in his appearance and liked things done in a certain way. At times he would get frustrated and swear... in Polish, because a nurse didn't know what he wanted. But Stan was a gentleman in all respects.*

This didn't match the information Mama had told me about Stan being drunk and violent. Sonia remembered that Stan did become angry at times because he was frustrated with his paralysis, but he always wanted to look presentable: *I remember when I would shave his face with the electric razor. He would always rub his face afterward, to make sure it was to his liking. He liked his hair combed and I could tell he was a proud man.* She concluded: *Overall I can tell you it was a pleasure taking care of him, as I look back he reminds me of my father. I wish I could speak Polish as I would have loved to have conversations with him. It was a pleasure taking care of him.*

Sonia painted a picture of a proud man struggling to come to terms with the stroke that disabled him at a relatively young age, who was fastidious about his appearance, a smoker, sharing a room—but very little conversation—with two other guys. After seventy years, this was a positive picture of the last years of my father's life. I am grateful to Sonia.

Eight months after our road trip to Kirkland Lake, Dave Pearce sent me a photo. The headstone I had ordered for Stan had been put in place. I called the florist and arranged for silk red and white flowers—the colours of the Polish and Canadian flags—to be placed on his grave every spring and summer. Stan would no longer languish in an unmarked grave.

So was this the end of my search? My head said yes, but my heart disagreed. I was the sum of two parts. I had followed Mama's story through her letters and my trip to

Germany. I understood the experiences that shaped her life, and I now felt a sense of peace with myself.

But what about my father? I had two conflicting stories about him. Sonia's recollections of his last years were different from Mama's recollection of his earlier years. Who was the real Stan? The POW? The man Mama met and fell in love with after the war? The logger? The abuser? The man in the Chateau? I needed to find out more. And I couldn't rest until I put a face to the man who had held me so lovingly while I clutched my little stove that Christmas in Timmins so long ago.

The answers, I was convinced, lay in Poland.

Dear Stan,

This is the most difficult letter I've ever written, because for so long I was so angry with you. But now I no longer want to give you a piece of my mind. I want to tell you what's in my heart.

And, oh, my heart still hurts. In all your life, you never came to find me. Why? Was I so bad? Did you never love me? Or did you think I was Frank's child, not yours?

Stan, I AM your daughter. I was only four years old when Mama and I left you. What happened between you and her was not my fault! You screwed up my relationships with men because I equated loving me with leaving me. I didn't care how messed up you were; you should have looked for me, Stan!

In my early twenties, I started looking for you. I was living in Sudbury. Twice I drove to Timmins to find you, but I was always turned back by some force of nature.

When I moved to Vancouver, then Montreal and London, England, I stopped looking for you. In my fifties, I moved to

Nova Scotia, and I started searching again. I told Mama, and she made me swear if I ever found you I would never tell you where she was. She said you were a "terrible man and often we had to run for our lives because of your drunken rages." Was that true, Stan? Or was that just Mama manipulating me as she probably manipulated you?

I can believe that you drank, though. Nobody spoke of post-traumatic stress disorder in your day, but if ever there was a candidate for PTSD, it was you. You were taken prisoner at the beginning of the war and shipped off to POW camps in Germany for the next five years. I can't imagine how you survived in those camps. But you did. I'm so proud of you.

And how did you survive in Canada after Mama and I left you? Did you retreat deeper into the woods, deeper into yourself? And what happened when you had that first stroke? You were still young, but your right arm and leg were paralyzed, so how could you work?

My heart broke when I saw the makeshift memorial to a broken life at your unmarked grave in the Kirkland Lake cemetery. I didn't think I would, but I cried and cried. Did my tears reach you?

Oh, Stan, I no longer blame you for not looking for me. You had your demons, just like Mama and Frank. I understand that now.

You will not be forgotten or abandoned again.

I will always remember you.

I love you,

Halina

Chapter 28

Poland

On a whim, I sent an email to the municipal offices in the village of Nienalty, in northeast Poland, where my father was born. I asked if anyone might remember any Żebrowskis, or if there was a local historian who might help me.

To my amazement, a Janusz Żebrowski replied. It turned out his grandfather had been my father's brother. So Janusz was my father's family, my family. I couldn't believe my good luck.

Janusz sent pictures of my paternal grandparents, Ignacy and Józefa, and pictures of the old family farmstead where my father grew up. I pored over them for hours, especially the pictures of my grandparents, trying to detect any family resemblance.

It was difficult communicating with Janusz. He spoke no English, and my Polish was almost non-existent. I had so many questions! But I was frustrated I couldn't get many answers. Luckily, Janusz told his mother, Regina, about me, and Regina told her youngest son.

On October 14, 2023, everything changed when I got an email in English from Janusz's younger brother. *My name is Krzysztof Żebrowski,* he wrote, *and my grandfather's brother was Stanisław. He was your birth father. It is my utmost pleasure to meet you virtually!*

Kris was in his thirties, worked in HR for a large international company, and spoke many languages. We had a three-hour video call to get acquainted. It was the most important and magical moment of my life—finding a family member and building a close relationship with him. We continue to email, text, or talk almost every day.

Kris, I learned, was the family historian. He had looked for me when he was about thirteen for a school project on family history. His curiosity was piqued by stories of a mysterious great-uncle who had gone missing in Canada after the war and had a daughter there. Because I had changed my name so often, Kris had been unable to find me.

Four more Żebrowskis contacted me that October. As an early Christmas present, I was discovering I was part of not only a large family but also a prestigious one.

My grandmother Józefa Żebrowska was born a Skłodowska and, according to many family members, was related to the Nobel Prize–winning physicist and chemist Marie Skłodowska-Curie. My jaw dropped.

And then another bombshell. My first cousin Kazimiera wrote: *I am in possession of a document from 1850, issued by the Heraldry of the Kingdom of Poland in the Płock Governorate, stating that Ignacy Żebrowski of the Jasieńczyk coat of arms and his descendants belong to a noble family.* My family had been part of Polish nobility since 1651. We were minor nobles, but still, we had a coat of arms. They were prosperous landowners and civic-minded individuals.

Why had Mama never told me? As the emails flew between the Żebrowskis and me, another one of Mama's deceits was revealed. Whenever I had asked Mama what her father, Sergei, did, she said he was a lieutenant in Tsar Nicholas II's army and that he was in the cavalry. Now I found out it was my paternal grandfather, Ignacy, who was a bodyguard in Moscow for Tsar Nicholas II, and my father was part of the Polish cavalry. Mama had stolen bits from Stan's and Ignacy's lives to weave a counterfeit identity for her father. Why? Was she ashamed Sergei worked in the forest in a worker's co-operative? I'll never know.

My grandfather Ignacy was an educated man. When he finished his service to the tsar, he married Józefa. He served in World War I, was captured, and subsequently escaped. He returned home to run the family farm and served as the mayor of his community.

My Żebrowski family sent me photos and told me family stories. I lingered over every picture and relished every story. I was in love with all of them. Only one thing was missing—a picture of my father.

With every email from my family, the more answers I got, the more questions I had. It was clear I had to go to Poland. Maybe by the time I got there, someone would have found a photograph of Stanisław.

To prepare my family to meet me, I sent them a short video of my story and included a picture taken at Christmas 1947, in the displaced persons camp in Weiden, Germany. On the left side of the photograph, Frank Użarowski, who later became my stepfather, sat looking at the camera. My mother was beside him with me, ten months old, on her lap. The right side of the picture was cut out. Mama had cut Stan out of every picture.

THREE WEEKS BEFORE NEIL and I were to leave for Poland, my phone pinged with an email from another Janusz Żebrowski, this one my first cousin. I opened it and burst into tears. I was looking at my father's face. It was the complete version of the Christmas photo—a clear shot of my father, Stanisław Żebrowski, sitting to the right of my mother and me.

I couldn't stop sobbing. I couldn't stop scrutinizing the picture. It was the eternal love triangle. Frank, my stepfather, gazing innocently at the camera with his arm around my mother. Stanisław, my father, the older man, looking out warily. The prize between them, my beautiful mama, with me squirming to get off her lap.

After more than seventy years, I was looking at the face of the man who married my mother in Germany after they both had survived desperately hard times in World War II. The man who, like my mother, turned his back on homeland and family to make a new start in Canada.

I discovered later that my father had sent a duplicate of the picture to his brother, Janusz's father, with whom he'd always had a good relationship. Janusz promised more pictures and letters when we got to Poland.

But meeting and thanking Janusz would have to wait. The first family member I met when I arrived in Warsaw was Ewa, my first cousin once removed, and her husband, Mariusz. They came to our hotel, and as soon as I saw her coming down the hallway, I ran into her arms. I could barely see her, I was crying so hard. I held her tight. All those years when I thought I had no one faded away in her arms.

At lunch, I caressed her cheek. "You have such lovely skin," I said.

"All Żebrowski women have good skin," she replied, touching my cheek in return. That gesture resonated. I was a Żebrowski woman. I was part of this family.

After Ewa, I met my first cousin Kazimiera Rząca, my father's niece, a distinguished woman four years older than me, and the matriarch of our family, the oldest living Żebrowski. Although Kazimiera still enjoyed good health, she, like many Poles, had already booked a spot in the family cemetery. Her tombstone is inscribed with her personal details and awaits the day of her death. But it's an unusual tombstone because inscribed at the top is: *In memory of Stanisław Żebrowski, son of Ignacy, soldier of the defensive war of 1939. Emigrant of war. Stayed to the end of his days in a foreign land.* Kazimiera chose to share her gravestone with my father, the uncle she never met. She didn't want him to be forgotten. I love her for this generous gesture. So Stan has two graves, one in Poland and one in Canada.

I told Kazimiera Mama's story about having to run from Stan because of his abusive, drunken rages. Kazimiera was incensed. "There's no way he would have been brought up to do something like that. No! Grandfather Ignacy was a gentle and kind man. He brought up Stan properly. Certainly not to be violent! My mother was married to Stan's brother. She talked a lot about Stanisław because they were peers; they were of a similar age. He was a very balanced man, very calm," Kazimiera assured me. "He was a kind man who would give you his last crust of bread, or the shirt off his back. I simply don't believe what your mother said."

Neither of us can claim to know the absolute truth of what happened between Mama and Stan. But whenever I was able to get Mama to talk about Stan, she always said he would drink heavily and abuse her. Sometime in the late 1950s, Stanisław stopped writing to his family. They tried, without success, to trace him through the Polish Red Cross. Both Kazimiera and I shed tears as we spoke of the impact of those events so many years ago.

But there were opportunities to laugh too. Kazimiera and her daughter Bozena arranged for a private tour of the Island Palace in Łazienki Park. It was the playground of former Polish King Stanisław August. The palace contains the king's private theatre, still in regular use today. Our guide led us through a door, and we found ourselves backstage, looking out at the opulent auditorium. Impulsively, I grabbed Kazimiera's hand. We ran out to centre stage like children and bowed deeply to our imaginary standing ovation. Finally, at eighty-one and seventy-seven years of age, my cousin and I let go of the past. The years slipped away, and we just played together.

When I met my other first cousin Krystyna and her daughter Malgorzata, Krystyna told me that all family Christmases had been tinged with sorrow because my father wasn't there, and because no one knew what had happened to him.

As for Stan being violent, Malgorzata told me, "It's possible to be one thing to your friends and relatives and another to your wife and child." Malgorzata, a doctor, agreed that—given what Stan went through in the POW camps—he very likely suffered from PTSD. Like other former POWs, he may have taken refuge in the bottle and taken out his frustrations on Mama. So it's possible both Mama and Kazimiera's versions are true, at least in part.

Finally, I met Kris. I wept with joy. He called me *ciocia*—"auntie" in Polish. I was touched and honoured. Before Kris, I was nobody's aunt.

Kris had a present for me—a cheery old-fashioned Christmas card my father had sent from Canada to his family in Poland in the late 1950s. The card made me sad. My father wished his family a Merry Christmas and all the best for the New Year. Then he signed it formally, S. Żebrowski. I ran my fingers over his name. No other signatures, and no mention of Mama or me.

What was that Christmas like for him? He was in a big country. He didn't speak much English. Did he spend the holiday with anyone? I don't know the real story behind the card, but I am content to think that, fifty or sixty years ago, someone in the Żebrowski family in Poland was so happy to receive the card that they stored it away with other family treasures. And I am so glad Kris found the card and gifted it to me.

Kris also gave me an experience I will never forget. He took me to my father's home. It's an old wooden house with shutters on the windows. This was where my father played with his brothers and sisters. Where he worked in the fields with my grandfather. The home he left for a war he never wanted. The home he never saw again. Nobody lives there anymore, just the family ghosts.

As I walked through the door into the old kitchen, I leaned against a dusty wall and wept. The old Żebrowski farmhouse was alive with memories. The old stove where the family baked bread was covered with dust. The latches on the doors were the ones my father would have touched. There were pictures of the Virgin Mary and Jesus on the wall. Tattered sheer curtains hung in the windows. The plaster was crumbling from the walls, but some of the decorations were unchanged from the days when Stan was growing up there.

I felt the house had waited for me to find it. It was filled with my father's spirit. I felt close to him. I thought, *We are both at peace.*

Kris, Ewa, and other Żebrowskis organized a big

family reunion at a hotel near the old house. I finally met Janusz, who had given me the picture of my father. He had more surprises for me: photocopies of four letters my father wrote to Janusz's father. The two men wrote to each other a few times in the 1950s. Correspondence was difficult, because while my father was in Canada, his brother, Janusz's father, was behind the Iron Curtain in Poland. Letters were read by the Soviets and sometimes lost.

The letters paint a picture of my father as a kind, caring man who tried to do what he could for his family and friends back in Poland. But they also portray Stan's slide from excited newlywed and would-be emigrant to bitter, jilted victim of a love triangle.

It all started innocently at the La Guardia DP camp in Weiden. Stan wrote to his brother:

As for me, for now, life is going smoothly, no worries. We are in good health, and wishing you the same. Franciszek Użarowski is still with me. It feels fine and fun with him around, but, for sure, not for long anymore. He's leaving soon. He has been accepted by Canada ... I am glad he's taking me along. I have passed the assessment too, but, at this time, I must wait, because the singles have the priority. I am sending you lots of greetings and kisses.

Always your loving,

Maria, Halina, and Stach

I noted the three names at the end, a sign of happier times. All the other letters are signed only S. Żebrowski or Stach. There is no further mention of Frank, because the unthinkable had happened: Stan was deceived by his countryman Frank, a man he liked. They were almost neighbours, both from villages in northeast Poland.

Three years after Mama ran off with Frank, Stan got the surprise of his life. He wrote to his brother in 1955:

As for my Madonna, she is roaming around Toronto. Recently I drove through Toronto. I even stayed three days, and I saw her, and she saw me. She wanted to walk up to me, but I didn't wait for her. I got in the car and drove off in another direction. Did she have such a bad life with me? Let her look for something better for herself.

Why were my mother and Stan in Toronto at the same time? Was Mama there with Walter, cheating on Frank? What were the chances of them running into each other? Did she try to make up with the man she told me was violent? Why did Stan walk away? Once again, I had no answers.

But I do know Stan loved his life as a logger in Canada. It was a hard life, cutting down trees and chopping them into logs in the dead of winter when temperatures ranged from -14 to -30 Celsius. He worked from sunrise to sundown, with Sundays off. In the summer he did odd jobs, which took him away from home for long stretches.

After Mama left him, he seemed to find solace in isolation. He found work in an even more remote part of Northern Ontario: Smooth Rock Falls, 100 kilometres north of Timmins. On September 15, 1955, Stan wrote to his brother:

This summer, for almost two months, I worked at forest fires. The job was quite good, well paid. As for me, I am in good health. *I work in the forest because this kind of job suits me best. Currently, I work with a chainsaw. This means cutting trees is easier by a half. I have locally everything except alcohol: that is strictly forbidden. Otherwise, I sleep very well.*

As well as loving the Canadian North, Stan loved his family. Probably more than ever after Mama had abandoned him. Stan's letter to his brother continued:

And now, my dears, don't feel uneasy and do let me know: maybe you need some stuff like clothes, shoes, etc.—let me know, and I'll do my best to send that to you.

He sent medicine, dress fabric, clothes, even a bicycle. He worried about the health of his parents, and who would take care of the family farm if anything happened to them. He worried about the health of friends, arranging shipments of antibiotics. A family story goes that someone told Stan that he should keep the money and gifts for himself because he needed them more than they did. Stan was offended. The letters stopped in 1956.

In Poland, I got a real sense of who my father was, especially from his letters. And thanks to Janusz, I had more pictures of my father. There he was, in his uniform with Mama on their wedding day. And a few years earlier, sitting with twenty-eight POWs around a table in a German prison camp at Christmas. There was food and drink on the table, but not one man was smiling. I think the picture was posed propaganda, because the back was stamped by the Nazis. There was an earlier picture of Stan as a handsome soldier in training, and finally one with Stan and five unidentified friends. I treasure them all and can't get enough of looking at them. I feel such gratitude to Janusz for giving me these treasures.

At the family reunion, Janusz and I danced together. The accordion player played the old Polish folk song "Mały biały domek." Mama had played that record all the time when I was growing up. I loved the song about a small white house where the singer was once happy because his beloved was there, but now she's gone and he has only memories.

As we danced, I saw my family around me. There were thirty Żebrowskis and Skłodowskis laughing and dancing. The table groaned with good Polish food. Wine, vodka, and beer made the rounds. The accordion player played Polish folk songs into the warm May night. I was in the arms of a man whom I had only met a few hours ago, yet I felt safe. I was happier than I had ever been in my life.

BEFORE NEIL AND I left Poland, we drove to a dirt parking lot shaded with large trees where we met Danuta, my stepfather Frank's niece. She guided us into a small cemetery and to the Użarowski family tombstone. Under photographs of his parents was a small image of Frank in a tuxedo, smiling at the camera. It had been taken on my wedding day to Neil. After Tata died, I had sent his ashes to Poland.

As I stood over his grave, I thought about our relationship. Was Frank a saviour who had rescued Mama and me from an abusive relationship? Or was he a double-crosser who betrayed his friend Stan by seducing his wife? Was I the price he was prepared to pay to have Mama for himself?

And, I wondered, was Frank swept up in Mama's intrigues and lies, or was he the one pulling the strings, controlling and manipulating us?

Toward the end of their lives, Mama and Frank had a strained relationship. They had gone from passionate love in their twenties to barely tolerating each other in their seventies. As their passion waned, Mama's complaints about Frank mounted: He wouldn't let her buy pretty things, he made her work hard, he wouldn't let her drive the car. With each complaint, Mama drew me tighter into her web. I always took her side in everything. I was her protector. I never considered Frank's side of the story. I'm sorry I never asked him about their relationship.

For all their complaining about each other, they could never live without each other, no matter how bad it became.

Once, I think Frank seriously imagined a life without Mama. He was seventy-three and made a surprise visit to Poland fifty years after the war. He had been threatening to leave Mama every time they fought, so he didn't take her to Poland with him. I believe he was planning to live there, but something happened and he returned to Canada earlier than expected. His brother said Frank had received a phone call from me in Canada and had to leave immediately, but I didn't call him. Something spooked him, and he came rushing back.

Frank was a complicated man. There were many contradictions in his life. For example, he hid money from Mama that I only discovered after his death, yet he bought me a new car after I moved back to Canada from England. Was that generosity or manipulation?

Frank's friendships and relationships were transactional: He would give you his time, or his honey or homemade wine, but he would always expect something in return.

Yet he was proud of me—of that I have no doubt—even though he could never tell me how he felt and rarely told me he loved me.

I wonder if he ever resented bringing up Stan's daughter. Did he ever feel guilty for taking me away from my father? I will never know. Frank clothed and fed me and provided a roof over my head. I'm grateful for that. The rest I did myself.

But still, I wonder: By telling me nothing about Stan, did he save me from my birth father or cost me the chance to have a loving relationship with him?

No matter what, when I went to Poland, a piece of a very big puzzle fell into place for me. I was no longer alone. I found my family, my ancestors, and my roots.

They would still be there when I returned to Canada. We would continue communicating and visiting. I realized family is everything. The Żebrowskis were blood of my blood. We were bound together. We shared a past, and we would share a future.

In Poland, the aching hole in my heart was healed.

Dear Grandfather Ignacy and Grandmother Józefa,
Grandfather Ignacy, when I saw your picture for the first time, I fell in love. It was the photo taken in Moscow in 1898, when you were twenty-two years old. You had been drafted into the Imperial Russian Army as a bodyguard at the Kremlin for Tsar Nicholas II.

I mooned over your picture like a schoolgirl. You were so handsome in your uniform. You looked like you could take on anything—and throughout your life, you did. When you left Moscow, the tsar gave you a beautiful jewelled Fabergé egg. It's still in the family.

You came home and married the love of your life. Grandmother Józefa, you were so sweet and diminutive standing alongside your tall, handsome soldier. It was a love match, wasn't it?

I visited the old farmstead where you raised your children. As I walked through its rooms, I heard the laughter of the kids, the clatter of their footsteps, and I felt the warmth of a loving family.

Grandmother, where was Grandfather when he told you he'd been called to fight in the Great War? In the house, or was it by that big old tree outside? Everyone seemed to love that tree. I imagine him taking your hand and kissing you before he left.

Grandfather, you fought in one of the first and biggest battles of World War I—the Battle of Tannenberg, on the side of the Russians against the Germans. It was your first battle. So many of your mates were killed or taken prisoner. The Germans caught you too, Grandfather, but you managed to escape, though it would be four years before you came home.

I can't help but note the parallel between you and your son—my father—Stanisław. He was captured in his first big battle in World War II—but he never could escape.

You were so much more than a soldier. When you came home, you were appointed mayor of your commune of fifteen villages. People loved and respected you. You were praised as a progressive thinker.

I wandered into the living room of your farmhouse. I saw the tattered curtain still hanging on the windows, paint peeling off the ceiling. I remembered the story of how you sheltered an elderly Jewish man in the attic from the Nazis.

The shadow of war was never far from you, was it? I didn't realize how close the farmhouse was to the Treblinka extermination camp—close enough for you to smell the smoke from the chimneys of death.

There were so many memories in that house. I looked at the old stove in the kitchen and recalled the story about Grandmother baking a "mouse" in her bread because you enjoyed it so much. The grandchildren thought you had lost your mind, until Grandmother took them aside and confessed the "mouse" was just a piece of ordinary meat baked in the bread. Oh, Grandfather Ignacy and Grandmother Józefa, how I wish I could have eaten your bread with the mouse and played at the farm with my cousins.

When I visited, I felt the peace of this magical corner of Poland. And I felt you both in my heart. I'm so grateful the family told me about you both, shared pictures, and took me to the house where you brought up my father.

My heart is full knowing I'm part of you, and that this will never change.

I love you both.

Your lost, but then found, granddaughter,

Halina

Chapter 29

A Final Boo

I had journeyed through Germany, Northern Ontario, and Poland in my quest to understand my mother, to find my father, and to discover my family. I learned a lot, but I was also left with many unanswered questions. I'm okay with that. After all, as the old saying goes, it's not about the destination; it's about the journey. It's what you discover along the way.

My discoveries began with my mother's death and an act of forgiveness. The last time I saw Mama was at the nursing home in Halifax. She was in bed, her eyes closed, her breathing laboured. She was in the fetal position, which was unusual. She always slept on her back.

"She's okay. She's just sleeping," said the young care assistant.

I knew something was wrong. I called our doctor and friend, Bharti Verma. Neil went down to the lobby to wait for her. I was alone with Mama. I knew she was dying.

I took her hand. She looked so tiny and frail in the bed, lying on her side, facing me. I thought about what we had, and what we lost. Our mother–daughter relationship had deteriorated as the years went by.

When I was a child, she was my beautiful Mama. I adored her. I always supported her, always took her side, especially in arguments with Tata, and always did what she told me.

As I grew older, our roles reversed. I became her mother. She relied on my opinion more and more. I tried to help her, woman-to-woman, but there were certain things she clung to, like never leaving Tata despite all the complaining she did about him. In the preceding fifteen years, she had become needier, more demanding.

I still loved her, but I knew, for my own sanity, I couldn't give her unfettered access to my heart and the power to control my life.

In her eyes, nothing that happened in her life had ever been her fault. She never took responsibility for her actions or their consequences. She would blame everyone, anyone, even me sometimes. I would console myself that this was the dementia speaking.

We needed boundaries, but setting them was painful. When she was depressed, she would lash out. Inevitably, her target would be me. Sometimes, when we were both frustrated, we would end up screaming at each other.

I took care of her, but I didn't care for her in the way she wanted. I became immune to her constant pleas for my attention. I managed her affairs—she was well looked after materially—but that was it.

But I didn't want her to die, and I didn't want to hold a lump of bitterness in my heart after she died. *It's not too late*, I thought as I sat holding her hand.

"Oh, Mama, I forgive you for everything you have done to hurt me," I whispered softly. "I know you didn't mean it. And please, please, forgive me for everything I did to hurt you. I didn't mean it, either." I squeezed her hand. I wanted her to know I was a good daughter, her daughter. I wanted to help her pass in love.

"If you need to go now, you can, Mama. It's all right. I will miss you. I want you to know I will never forget you. Never. I love you. I never stopped loving you. I know you did your best. I know it was hard. You can rest now. You will always, always be my beautiful Mama."

I believe she heard me.

When Bharti arrived, she raised the bed and moved Mama into a sitting position so she could breathe more easily. Through all of this, Mama never opened her eyes. We waited.

It wasn't long before Mama took a long, deep breath. The sound of her breathing filled the room. She took a second breath with the same intensity. Then a third. I knew she was fighting to live. I felt the power of the moment. I was both scared and honoured to be there.

We waited for a fourth breath, but it never came.

I didn't cry. I reached over and removed the gold and opal earrings I had given her that she never took off.

We had her cremated. There was no service, and no one came to the funeral home. It was so different from

Tata's well-attended funeral in St. Catharines and Aniela's opulent one in Vinnytsia. In her short time in Halifax, Mama had alienated the few friends she had. When I saw her in the coffin for the last time, I was struck by how small and childlike she looked. But I didn't cry.

After she was cremated, the funeral director put her urn into an emerald-green velvet pouch with a gold cord and handed it to me. I still didn't cry. I placed the urn in the closet in Neil's office. I didn't want to see it until I figured out what to do with it.

EIGHTEEN MONTHS LATER, on a summer's day in August, Neil and I took Mama's urn and motored out in a friend's boat with two neighbours to a small island in Mahone Bay. We anchored in clear turquoise waters under a blue sky. The water danced with diamonds.

I clutched Mama's biodegradable sand urn in both hands on the platform at the back of the boat. The urn had a lid that looked like a big mushroom cap. I had opened it once at home and looked at the bag with Mama's ashes. I had put my hand inside and felt the bag, trying to connect with the ashes. I hadn't cried then, either.

But as I knelt on the boat and held the urn between my knees, a sob escaped from somewhere deep inside. My eyes blurred. I began wailing, howling like a wounded animal.

I cried for my Mama, for what could have been, should have been, between us but never was. I wept for her pain, for my pain. I wept angry tears for the war that tore her life apart and dictated at least part of mine. I wept because I still loved her. Despite everything, she was my Mama. My beautiful Mama.

I rocked on my heels, clutching her urn to my chest. I couldn't let her go. Not just yet. I don't know how long I cried, but finally my sobs turned into teary hiccups. I lowered the urn into the water. I still couldn't let it go. The water was cold. My fingers were freezing.

All I could do was whisper "Oh, Mama, Mama, Mama."

Finally, I took a deep breath and released Mama into the ocean. The urn sank quickly, more quickly than I expected. I leaned over the water to watch it drop.

Suddenly, the lid shot back up to the surface with such force it made a loud pop and almost hit me in the face. I stopped crying mid-sob and stared in amazement as the lid of the urn settled alongside the boat. Then I started to laugh. I couldn't stop. Everyone joined in.

Oh, Mama, you just had to have the last word.

Mama was playing with me, even then, trying to scare me the way she used to when I was young. Whenever I had the hiccups, Mama would sneak behind me and shout "Boo!" This was her last "boo."

I felt close to her in that moment. I felt that my real Mama, the one I had longed for all my life, was speaking to me now.

Don't be sad, Halina. Don't cry. You're going to be all right.

A wave danced the lid away. We scattered roses after it, then daisies. As the current caught the lid, the roses, like scarlet soldiers, lined up behind it and followed. The daisies fanned out in a V shape behind the roses. We watched this strange little procession drift away with the waves until we could see it no more. Then we cracked open the champagne and raised a toast in her memory.

As we motored back, I thought, *Yes, Mama was the survivor she always said she was.* I had so often dismissed her claim. Now I knew she was right. She had survived the war, and she had survived failed marriages, failed businesses, and failed relationships.

The only thing she didn't totally fail at was me. She gave me all the necessities of life—food, water, and shelter—but not the love I craved. She was determined not to spoil me like Sergei and Aniela had spoiled her. She withheld love. She didn't really know how to give me love. Neither did Frank. But somehow, between the two of them, they managed to bring up an independent woman who made a success of her life.

Until I found her letters, I had no idea of how little I knew about my mother's past. I had no idea how much despair and deception there'd been in her life. And I had no idea what discoveries lay ahead of me as I searched for the truth.

I am so thankful I didn't toss the letters out. They gave me a new appreciation for my mother's grit and stamina. They led me to my father's grave, and his story. Yes, I will always have questions about why he never came for me. But that was his journey, his decision, not mine.

And I see Tata in a different light too. He betrayed my father in the name of love. How did he feel bringing up

Stan's daughter? It must have been so difficult for him to see me every day and not be reminded of the past.

The letters helped me know and better understand Aniela and Sergei, their joy at having their golden daughter, and their excruciating pain at losing her.

Through my journey I have seen and felt in my heart the courage and fortitude of Mama, Stan, Frank, Aniela, and Sergei. And I've also learned of their flaws and deceptions. I don't blame them for anything. They were only human.

The most important gift from this journey has been finding my family in Poland. I see parallels between my maternal grandparents, Aniela and Sergei, and my paternal grandparents, Ignacy and Józefa: the loss of a child to war, the relief at the discovery the child was alive, and then the sorrow at realizing that child was never coming home.

I have learned much on my journey. I have answered some of the questions that have haunted me all my life. I have found my father. I have found a family—my family—blood of my blood. And through them, I have found love that I never knew I had.

Acknowledgements

Writing can be a solitary adventure at times, but researching the story—especially when some of the characters did their best to keep their secrets hidden—involves a great team effort. So I cannot end this book without acknowledging the people who were instrumental in helping me tell my tale.

I am so thankful and grateful that my husband, Neil Everton, was at my side every step of the way. Neil, a brilliant producer and editor, was the first reader of anything I wrote. I cannot thank him enough for his wise counsel. He is my rock and my North Star.

I would also like to thank Anna Maria Tremonti. As a close friend, she knew my mother and my stepfather. Once she had read some of my mother's letters, she was the first to tell me this was a book, and I had to write it.

I am so grateful to my editor, Shirarose Wilensky of House of Anansi. I was introduced to her when I was halfway through my book. I asked her about finding an agent or a publisher. She listened intently as I told her my story. Finally she said, "I think I want you for myself." I was ecstatic. Her editing advice was brilliant, her structural suggestions spot-on, and her support unflagging. I can't believe how lucky I was to have her expertise and enthusiasm on my side.

I had never worked with a publisher, never mind such a distinguished one as House of Anansi. I would like to thank Melissa Shirley, Emma Rhodes, Alysia Shewchuk, Jenny McWha, Tracy Bordian, Sue Sumeraj, and all the other professionals at Anansi who helped with this book.

I would like to thank Marina Pereslavtseva, a tailor like my grandmother, who first translated my mother's letters—fifty-five in all. When she returned them, she said they had brought her to tears.

I sent the letters to Michael Kramer, a retired translator for the Canadian government. Michael came from the same area of Ukraine as my mother. Not only did he know the linguistic idiosyncrasies in the letters, but he also provided invaluable insight and historical context. I thank him so much for his wisdom, and for his patience with my endless questions.

I thank the team at the Arolsen Archives (International Center on Nazi Persecution) in Germany, who provided me with critical documents regarding my mother's time as a Nazi slave worker.

My sincere thank you to Bad Reichenhall city archivist Dr. Johannes Lang for his advice, and for arranging a tour of Camp Hope, now a German military base. There I met

Lieutenant Colonel Thomas Nockelmann, the commander of the base, who patiently answered my questions and gave me many valuable insights into the war period. I am indebted to him.

Lieutenant Colonel Nockelmann connected me to Bernard Dichek, a journalist and documentary filmmaker in Tel Aviv whose parents had been in Camp Hope. Bernard generously shared his research with me.

Thank you to Captain Michael Nadolski, of the military base in Bad Reichenhall, who endeavoured to find the places in the town and along the Saalach River that appeared in old family pictures.

Thank you to archivist Dr. Sebastian Schott in the city of Weiden, where I was born. He shared maps of the DP camp and helped me find my parents' marriage documents and certificate.

Thank you to Frau Irmgard Schwindl of the Herz Jesu church in Weiden. She found my baptismal records and told me about my godfather.

Thank you to Werner Enke of the Initiative Against Forgetting in Schweinfurt for taking me to the memorial walk where my mother's barracks once stood when she was a slave worker in the ball-bearing factories, and for sharing stories of other slave workers.

Thank you to historian Alexander Kraus of the Stolpersteine (Stumbling Stones) Project in Würzburg, Germany. Alex not only took me to the house where my mother worked as a housemaid but also patiently answered countless emails.

Thank you to Würzburg city archivist Christian Kensy, Neumarkt archivist Petra Henseler, and Benita Stolz, one of the initiators of the Stolpersteine Project.

I would like to thank Sonia Pietrasik-Lang for nursing my birth father through his last years at the Chateau Nursing Home in Kirkland Lake, Ontario, and for sharing her memories of the man he was then.

Thank you to Orest Lawryniw for telling me about the life of DPs in Timmins, Ontario, and to Karina Douglas-Takayesu of the Timmins Public Library and Kaitlyn McKay of the Museum of Northern History in Kirkland Lake. And thank you to Dave Pearce at Swastika Cemetery in Kirkland Lake for finding my father's unmarked grave.

I would like to thank the unknown individual at the Zareby Koscielne Municipal Office in Poland who received a speculative inquiry from a stranger in Canada and took the trouble to share it with a member of the Żebrowski family.

A profound thank you to my newfound family in Poland, who embraced me unconditionally and told me many stories about the family and my father: Krzysztof Żebrowski, Ewa and Mariusz Wienko, Kazimeria Rzaca, Bozena Rzaca, Malgorzata Socik-Pojawa, Krystyna Socik, Wlodzimierz and Regina Żebrowski, and Janusz and Barbara Żebrowski.

Thank you to Marcin and Emilia Senderski in Poland, who found me through a genealogical site and are part of the Sklodowski branch of my family.

Thank you to historian Dr. Jan Raska in Halifax for

helping me understand what it was like to immigrate to Canada in the 1950s via Pier 21.

My deep gratitude to Sharon Jessup-Joyce and Brian Callahan, who formed a three-person memoir group with me and got me going. Their feedback was invaluable.

When I began this book, I knew nothing about my maternal grandparents or my birth father. I had letters, and birth and death dates. I asked Deborah Young, a gifted astrologer, and Faith Wood, a handwriting expert, what these clues told them about my father and grandparents. Their interpretations gave me a glimpse into personalities that were later mostly confirmed by the letters and documents.

A heartfelt thank you to my friend and therapist Faythe Buchanan. Not only did she help me make sense of the emotions in some of the letters, but she also kept me from falling apart as I dealt with many painful memories of my mother and my sense of abandonment by my father.

I want to thank my circle of close friends who have patiently helped me navigate the highs and lows of writing this book. They cheered me on through my discoveries, and perhaps more importantly, they supported me when the emotional toll of some of those discoveries became a little hard to bear.

I am so grateful to everyone for helping me tell a story that needed to be told.

HALINA ST. JAMES was a journalist for the CBC and CTV, covering revolutions, a war, election campaigns, and three Olympics. Later, she became a performance coach for business and government leaders. Halina lives in Nova Scotia.